Essential
Garden
Answers

Essential Garden Answers

Expert Answers To Over 300 Questions

Stefan Buczacki

TED SMART

Executive Editor: Julian Brown
Creative Director: Keith Martin
Design Manager: Bryan Dunn
Senior Designer: Peter Burt
Design: Les Needham
Picture Researcher: Christine Junemann
Production Controller: Louise Hall
Illustrator: Damien Rochford

First published in Great Britain in 2000 by Hamlyn, a division of
Octopus Publishing Group Limited, 2–4 Heron Quays, London, E14 4JP

This edition produced for
The Book People Ltd
Hall Wood Avenue, Haydock, St Helens
WA11 9UL

ISBN 0 600 60368 7

A CIP catalogue record of this book is available from the British Library.

Printed in China

Contents

Introduction

I am certain that ever since people first began to garden, they have wanted answers to questions. Of course, gardening isn't unique in that respect but this is a subject where the question and answer format has become a truly central feature. This surely is why 'Gardeners' Question Time', rather than 'DIY Question Time' or 'Cooks' Question Time' endured on the radio.

Trying to solve gardeners' problems and so help them gain more enjoyment from the subject that so fascinates me has been a central part of my life for a great many years. I think I have probably met more gardeners and answered more of their questions, certainly on radio and television, than anyone else in the country. It's a matter of fact that I have appeared on 'Gardeners' Question Time' on BBC Radio 4 more times than any other contributor and, when over 600 of these programmes are added to around 150 'Classic Gardening Forum' shows on Classic FM and many hundreds of television appearances, it does all represent a substantial body of questions.

Over the years, I have made copious notes to keep me abreast of the types of problem that have been prevalent at particular times and to see how gardening trends change. It's from these many thousands of questions that I have selected the 300 or so that appear in this book. They are, therefore, real questions, asked by real gardeners with real problems and anxieties, and I have selected those that I believe will have a particularly wide general appeal.

I have divided the questions along fairly conventional lines, into Fruit, Lawns, Vegetables and so forth, although much of the advice does cut across subject boundaries. I hope that you will enjoy reading the book for its own sake, not simply to find the solution to a particular problem.

Wherever possible, I have chosen questions that have 'hidden depth', questions that don't always produce the most obvious, or even an obvious answer. I have elaborated wherever feasible in the manner that I have found gardeners appreciate: to explain why I am giving a particular response or recommending a particular solution. It's been a guiding principle of my own gardening and also my professional career that understanding is not only the key to success, it's also the key to better enjoyment of your subject. I like to send a questioner away not just satisfied that he or she knows how to proceed but fired with the enthusiasm to put the advice into practice.

To be able to advise others meaningfully, you need yourself to have gardened winter and summer over many years. To understand what real gardening is about, to appreciate what real gardeners need to know, a gardening expert should live, sleep, eat and breathe his own garden. He should wake up to his frosted leeks, see the sun rise over a dew-sodden lawn and realize that it will be too wet to mow before midday, know what it means to have to put fleece over his tender seedlings last thing at night in late May, pause to regret not having sprayed his potatoes against blight and wonder why his apples have more codling moth in them this year than last – he should, quite simply, garden. I think I can say that I have done that and I hope you enjoy sharing a little of what I have gained.

Finally, however, may I finish with a simple thought? It's good that gardeners want to ask questions of experts and I hope that they may long continue to do so. But I hope also that everyone will want to build on this advice through accumulating their own fund of knowledge. Study and guidance can take you so far but above all, gardening is a subject where ultimately your own experience will be crucial. I have said many times that I never go into my own garden without learning or seeing something that I have never known or seen before. I hope that you will do the same; that you will garden with your eyes open and your mind receptive to the wonders that this enduringly satisfying pursuit can bring.

Annuals &
biennials

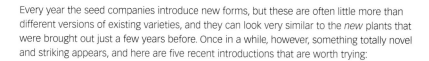

What is the difference between annuals, biennials and half-hardy plants?

ABOVE: The most attractive bedding displays are generally achieved with a mixture of hardy and half-hardy plants.

An annual is a plant that completes its life cycle from seed to seed within one season – that is, it is sown as a seed, flowers, sets seed and dies within a single year. *Lathyrus odoratus* (sweet pea) and clarkias are annuals. Some plants, such as some types of lobelia and *Rudbeckia hirta* (black-eyed Susan), which are really perennials and are capable of lasting for many years, perform better in a garden if they are treated like annuals and sown afresh each season.

A biennial is a plant that requires two seasons in which to complete its life cycle – that is, it establishes itself in the first year and then flowers and sets seed in the second year before dying. *Digitalis* spp. (foxglove) are biennials.

A half-hardy plant is one that can be grown outdoors in summer but should not be planted or sown outside until all danger of frost has passed because it will not withstand temperatures lower than 0°C (32°F). *Tagetes* spp. (French and African marigolds) are half-hardy. A hardy plant, on the other hand, is one that is capable of surviving outdoors with no artificial protection.

Are there some new annual bedding plants that I can use to make my border look a bit different from usual?

Every year the seed companies introduce new forms, but these are often little more than different versions of existing varieties, and they can look very similar to the *new* plants that were brought out just a few years before. Once in a while, however, something totally novel and striking appears, and here are five recent introductions that are worth trying:

* *Asarina procumbens* (climbing snapdragon) is available with white, red or purple flowers and is excellent for hanging baskets.
* *Brachyscome iberidifolia* (Swan River daisy) is available in a stunning new range of much stronger-growing varieties.
* *Heteropappus altaicus* is a glorious, compact, blue daisy that flowers in autumn. There is something about blue daisies that gardeners seem to find irresistible.
* *Impatiens auricoma* is the parent plant of several varieties of yellow-flowered busy Lizzie.
* *Scaevola aemula* (fairy fan-flower) produces beautiful and long-lasting, fan-shaped purple flowers on a neatly cascading plant.

Which annuals or biennials can be relied on to give colour to beds and borders early in the season?

It is in the early part of the season that biennials really come into their own because they have a considerable head-start over any annual, no matter how early it is sown. Two of the best biennials are *Erysimum cheiri* (wallflower) and *Dianthus barbatus* (sweet William).

Wallflowers are now available in far fewer varieties than a few years ago, but there are still several reliable tall-growing and dwarf bedding varieties for you to choose from. Look out for 'Harpur Crewe', which has yellow flowers in spring, and 'Bowles' Mauve', which bears mauve flowers from early spring to autumn.

Although they flower later than most wallflowers, sweet Williams have long been cottage garden favourites, and 'Indian Carpet' is one of the neatest and most compact varieties of all, with crimson, purple and pink flowers from late spring to early summer.

The annuals that give the best flowers in the early part of the year are those that are tough enough to have been sown the previous autumn, and although they won't have had as long to grow as the biennials, they will also be approaching flowering by early spring. The following are worth growing:

- ❀ *Calendula officinalis* (marigold, pot marigold) is available with yellow or orange, double or semi-double cottage garden flowers.
- ❀ *Centaurea cyanus* (cornflower), once a common cornfield weed, has flowers of clear blue.
- ❀ *Clarkia amoena* (syn. *Godetia amoena*, *G.grandiflora*; satin flower) looks like miniature hollyhocks, with flowers in white or shades of pink, purple or red.

- ❀ *Consolida ajacis* (syn. *C. ambigua*, *Delphinium consolida*; larkspur) is a type of delphinium and will give height to the early-season border.
- ❀ *Echium vulgare* (viper's bugloss) is a biennial which is grown as an annual and bears spikes of blue, white and pink flowers.
- ❀ *Eschscholzia californica* (Californian poppy) has flowers in vivid shades of orange, yellow, red and pink and in white.
- ❀ *Gypsophila elegans* produces

masses of tiny, long-lasting white flowers.
- ❀ *Iberis umbellata* (candytuft) bears flattish heads of white, pink or lilac flowers.
- ❀ *Lobularia maritima* (alyssum) is dwarf and compact and is a good choice for edging.
- ❀ *Malcolmia maritima* (Virginia stock), an easy-to-grow plant, bears flowers in shades of red, pink, mauve and blue and in white.
- ❀ *Papaver somniferum* (poppy) produces beautiful, if short-lived, flowers in a range of brilliant colours.

ABOVE: *Eschscholzia*, the Californian poppy, is one of the stand-bys for early season colour in my own garden.

Which annuals will readily self-seed?

The following will all self-seed reliably and do not need renewing each year. But remember that any plant that self-seeds will grow where it wants to, not where you want it.

LEFT: A recent explosion in varieties has seen dwarf and tall nasturtiums in a wide colour range.

- ❀ *Borago officinalis* (borage)
- ❀ *Calendula officinalis* (marigold, pot marigold)
- ❀ *Iberis umbellata* (candytuft)
- ❀ *Tropaeolum* cvs. (nasturtium)
- ❀ *Viola tricolor* (heartsease)

- ❀ Finally, don't forget *Myosotis sylvatica* (forget-me-not), which is a biennial or short-lived perennial that is often treated as a self-seeding annual.

Which summer flowers are suitable for drying?

The best annuals to choose are those with flowers with a rather straw-like texture. They are known as everlasting flowers and are listed in catalogues under various names, notably *Bracteantha* (syn. *Helichrysum*) and *Rhodanthe*, which now includes *Acroclinium and Helipterum*. The familiar *Dimorphotheca* (African daisy) can be used, too. Other annuals that dry well, either as flowers or fruiting heads, are *Calendula* (marigold), *Celosia* (cockscomb), clarkia, dahlia (single-flowered forms), *Consolida ajacis* (larkspur), *Iberis umbellata* (candytuft), *Lunaria* (honesty), *Reseda* (mignonette), *Moluccella* (bells of Ireland), *Nigella* (love-in-a-mist), poppy, *Physalis alkekengi* (Chinese lantern), salvia and scabious. Some ornamental grasses, such as *Helictotrichon sempervirens* (blue oat grass) and *Briza* (quaking grass), are also suitable for drying.

Cut the plants in the morning, before the colours have faded in the sun but after morning dew has had a chance to dry, and select taller, longer-stemmed varieties. Only pick plants that are perfect and avoid those with large, showy flowers, big double flowers or weak and fragile petals. They will dry as poor shadows of their garden form, will fall apart once they have dried or they will rot.

The easiest way to dry annuals is to fasten the cut flowers in loose bunches and to hang them upside down in a warm, well-ventilated room.

ABOVE: Calendulas or pot marigolds were traditionally always orange but a wide colour range is now obtainable.

Is it better to buy my bedding plants or to raise my own?

Raising plants from seed is hugely satisfying, even if you have bought the seed in a packet, but it takes time and space, which few gardeners have in unlimited supplies. You are, in addition, unlikely to achieve results as good as those of a commercial plant raiser. On the other hand, of course, you will pay more to cover the nursery's own costs and to provide them with a profit.

Many gardeners find that it makes sense to buy the common bedding plants that are required in relatively large numbers, but that it is a better option to raise from seed plants that are needed in smaller numbers or uncommon types that are not widely available in garden centres. An increasingly popular half-way house is to buy small 'plantlets' or 'plugs', which are available for you to grow on to planting size. Here the biggest outlay of cost and time has already been done.

One great advantage of buying plants that are already in growth is that it is possible to see what colour the flowers will be, and if you are planning a complex bedding scheme this could be a deciding factor when you make your choice.

Is it worth saving seed of annuals to plant next year?

Yes, it is usually worth saving seed, but there are some occasions when you should not do so.

Do not save seed from plants you know to be F1 hybrids – that is, from plants that are first-generation crosses of two distinct, but closely related parents. Any seed you save from the hybrid is likely to result in plants that bear little resemblance to the seed parent. F1 hybrid seed must be raised afresh from new crossings each year, and for this reason it tends to be more expensive than other seed, but it will produce plants that look like those illustrated on the packets. Because they are bred to flower over a long period, some F1 hybrids are sterile and do not set any seed. An associated point is that you should never offer for sale any seed that you have saved because the cultivar may be legally protected by breeders' rights, which means that only the breeder who owns the rights to a particular cultivar is legally entitled to sell it.

Never save seed from plants that are sickly or abnormal because they may be diseased, and the disease could be passed on to the progeny.

Remember, too, that you should always store seed carefully. From one year to the next it can be kept most easily in small paper packets in a screw-top jar in the fridge.

Can you suggest some annuals that will grow successfully under trees and shrubs?

Few annuals are really successful in shade – think how few flowers there are in woods – but the following should do reasonably well:

* *Begonia semperflorens* Cultorum Group (fibrous-rooted begonia)
* *Collinsia bicolor*
* *Impatiens* (busy Lizzie)
* *Lobelia*
* *Nemophila* (Californian bluebell)
* *Nicotiana* (ornamental tobacco plant)

ABOVE: Although some of the colours may be strident, there's no denying the ability of busy Lizzies to thrive in shade.

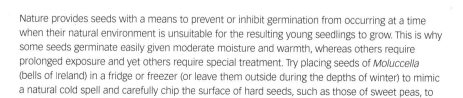

Why does seed of some bedding plants germinate more quickly than seed of other plants?

Nature provides seeds with a means to prevent or inhibit germination from occurring at a time when their natural environment is unsuitable for the resulting young seedlings to grow. This is why some seeds germinate easily given moderate moisture and warmth, whereas others require prolonged exposure and yet others require special treatment. Try placing seeds of *Moluccella* (bells of Ireland) in a fridge or freezer (or leave them outside during the depths of winter) to mimic a natural cold spell and carefully chip the surface of hard seeds, such as those of sweet peas, to encourage germination.

Remember, too, that some small seeds – lobelia and fibrous-rooted begonia, for example – contain insufficient food to enable the seedlings to reach the light if they are buried. These seeds should always be scattered thinly on the surface of the compost and kept just moist.

Are there any annuals that will give colour all summer long in hanging baskets and windowboxes?

Before you choose, remember that you usually look up towards a hanging basket but down on to a windowbox and it is important that both appear attractive from all angles for as long a period as possible. Ideally, you need to combine a selection of compact, trailing and climbing plants.

The following annuals and tender perennials that are grown as annuals will offer fairly good continuity, and the greater the number of varieties you can include, the better you will succeed.

	RECOMMENDED FOR	
GENUS	**HANGING BASKETS**	**WINDOWBOXES**
Ageratum	no	yes
Alyssum	no	yes
Anchusa	no	yes
Aster	no	yes
Begonia	yes	yes
Brachyscome	yes	yes
Browallia (bush violet)	yes	yes
Calceolaria (slipper flower)	yes	yes
Campanula (bellflower)	yes	yes
Convolvulus	yes	yes
Cuphea	yes	yes
Dianthus	yes	yes
Diascia	yes	yes
Eccremocarpus (Chilean glory flower)	yes	no
Erigeron (fleabane)	yes	no
Gazania	no	yes
Impatiens (busy Lizzie)	yes	yes
Lathyrus odoratus (dwarf sweet pea)	yes	yes
Lobelia	yes	yes
Mimulus	yes	yes
Nemesia	yes	yes
Nemophila	yes	yes
Nierembergia (cup flower)	yes	yes
Nolana	yes	yes
Pelargonium	yes	yes
Pericallis (syn. *Cineraria*)	yes	yes
Petunia	yes	yes
Schizanthus (butterfly flower)	no	yes
Solenostemon (syn. *Coleus*)	no	yes
Tagetes	no	yes
Thunbergia	yes	no
Tropaeolum	yes	no
Verbena	yes	yes
Viola	yes	yes

ABOVE: Night-scented stocks are among the more reliable, although far from the only night-scented annuals.

BELOW: Pansies, and to some extent other types of *Viola*, like these 'Huntercombe Purple', may fail to grow where similar plants have grown before.

Some of my wallflowers have pretty yellow stripes on the flowers. Have I created a new variety?

Sadly, no. The plants are contaminated with a virus that has caused this curious effect. It is known as 'flower breaking' and is also quite common on some types of tulip. When it affects wallflowers, the virus is called turnip mosaic virus, and the symptom is a reminder of the cross-infection by viruses that can occur between plants. This particular virus attacks not only wallflowers, but also turnips and other brassicas, so the attractive embellishment on the wallflowers may be a signal that your Brussels sprouts are already infected. A sensible vegetable gardener will uproot and destroy the 'new variety' of wallflowers before aphids transfer the virus to the family's greens.

Can you recommend some night-scented annuals for my garden?

There are many, but not many that are really hardy in gardens in Britain. The following are reliable, but remember that night-scented flowers are often white or otherwise unspectacular to look at during the day:

* *Hesperis matronalis* (dame's violet, sweet rocket)
* *Oenothera* (evening primrose)
* *Matthiola bicornis* (night-scented stock)
* *Nicotiana* (ornamental tobacco plant)
* *Reseda odorata* (mignonette)
* And for some good perennials, try phlox and honeysuckle.

How much care do bedding plants need apart from watering?

Regular feeding is essential. Plants that are in containers need a liquid feed at least once a week, and those in the open garden should be fed once every two weeks unless the soil is extremely fertile. Plants that are grown in containers, including hanging baskets and windowboxes, will benefit if slow-release fertilizer pellets are incorporated with the compost at planting time. Use the quantity recommended by the manufacturer.

Dead-heading is often overlooked, but it is important for larger-flowered varieties, although it is almost impossible with tiny-flowered types, such as lobelias and diascias.

Pansies refuse to grow in my garden. What am I doing wrong?

Probably nothing apart from trying to grow pansies where pansies have grown before. The problem is sometimes called replant disease or 'pansy sickness', and it is believed to be due to the build-up in the soil of a microscopic mould. A similar condition occurs with asters when they are grown repeatedly in the same spot, and roses are notorious for suffering from the problem.

If moving the pansies to a different part of the garden doesn't solve the problem, try growing them in containers, or raise them in small pots and then plant them out in the ball of pot compost. This will give the roots a contamination-free base, which should enable them to flower satisfactorily.

What easy-to-grow annuals are suitable for a child's first garden?

The one virtue that most young children lack is patience, so guide them towards plants that grow quickly and give results as dramatically and as soon as possible. Among the best:

* *Borago officinalis* (borage) is a bushy annual herb with masses of star-shaped, bright blue flowers.
* *Calendula* (marigold) has flowers in bright oranges and reds that can be added to salads.
* *Hibiscus trionum* (flower-of-an-hour) is a fast-growing annual that bears very short-lived individual flowers but blooms over a long period and produces attractive inflated seed pods.

* *Nemesia* bears small, trumpet-shaped flowers in a range of colours.
* *Nigella* (love-in-a-mist) has spiky, soft blue flowers of an individual shape.
* *Tithonia* (Mexican sunflower) bears masses of rich orange, daisy-like flowers over a long period on a 1m (3ft) high bushy plant.
* *Tropaeolum* (nasturtium) is available in both bushy and climbing forms, which have orange and red flowers.

tip

Sowing seed

Some seeds are so tiny that it is difficult to scatter them evenly. Mixing the seed with sharp sand makes it possible to achieve an even spread and also, when you are broadcast-sowing seed of plants such as *Borago officinalis* (borage) and *Limnanthes douglasii* (poached-egg plant), you can see where the seeds have fallen.

ABOVE: For perfume, I have no hesitation in saying that this ancestral type of sweet pea, 'Matucana', is peerless.

Is there an infallible method for growing sweet peas successfully?

The single most important factor is moisture. Dryness at the roots leads to poor flowering and is one of the conditions that predisposes the plants to mildew. Conversely, however, waterlogged soil will cause root rot, so good drainage is equally important. Prepare the planting site thoroughly in autumn by digging down to about 30cm (12in) and forking in plenty of garden compost and a scattering of bonemeal.

Position is important too, because sweet peas need sun and warmth. They also need support, and a wigwam of canes is ideal for normal gardens, although if you are growing for exhibition purposes you will probably use a cordon system.

Sweet peas are hardy and can be sown in autumn or spring outdoors or in a greenhouse. I usually sow in the greenhouse in late January or early February. I pinch out the tops, move them to a cold frame fairly swiftly and plant them outside at the beginning of April.

Which annuals will provide a good display of cut flowers in late summer?

Although the best display will always come from a blend of annuals and perennials, the following annuals should reliably be in flower in late summer, have good, long stems and will keep well when cut:

- *Alcea rosea* (syn. *Althaea rosea*; hollyhock)
- *Antirrhinum* (snapdragon)
- *Arctotis* (African daisy)
- *Bracteantha bracteata* (syn. *Helichrysum bracteatum*; strawflower, golden everlasting)
- *Calendula officinalis* (marigold, pot marigold)
- *Callistephus chinensis* (China aster)
- *Centaurea cyanus* (cornflower)
- *Chrysanthemum*
- *Clarkia amoena* (syn. *Godetia amoena, G. grandiflora*; satin flower)
- *Cleome hassleriana* (spider flower)
- *Consolida ajacis* (syn. *C.ambigua, Delphinium consolida*; larkspur)
- *Coreopsis tinctoria* (tickseed)
- *Cosmos bipinnatus* and *C. sulphureus*
- *Dahlia*
- *Gaillardia pulchella* (blanket flower)
- *Gazania*
- *Helianthus* (sunflower)
- *Lavatera* (mallow)
- *Nicotiana* (tobacco plant)
- *Rudbeckia hirta* (syn. *R. gloriosa*; black-eyed Susan)
- *Scabiosa stellata* (scabious)
- *Zinnia*

ABOVE: Although sunflowers have traditionally been single and tall, there are now dwarf and double-flowered varieties too.

What should I do with my bedding plants at the end of summer?

Although most summer bedding plants find their way to the compost heap, there are always a few that are worth potting up and bringing indoors to serve as colourful house plants for a few weeks. Plant them in slightly weak growing medium, such as John Innes No. 1.

Try saving pelargoniums, fuchsias and marguerites (which are really perennials anyway) together with the more compact types that have been raised from seed – busy Lizzies and fibrous-rooted begonias are among the best. The least successful are trailing plants, such as lobelias and *Brachyscome* (Swan river daisy), and those such as *Tagetes* (African and French marigold) and petunias, which are too large or unruly.

LEFT: The New Guinea hybrid busy Lizzies have as much to offer in foliage as in flower appeal and make excellent pot plants.

Perennials

I have heard it said that herbaceous borders are out of fashion. Is this true and, if it is, why?

ABOVE: The herbaceous border is a feature of great beauty in summer, but offers nothing in winter.

Traditionally, the herbaceous border contains a blend of plants of varying heights, spreads, flowering seasons and colours, usually in a relatively long and fairly narrow bed. The nature of the plants themselves tends to make this a labour-intensive arrangement, requiring routine staking and dead-heading. This was not, of course, a problem for Victorian garden-owners, who had gardeners to do all the work, and it may be appropriate today for people with large gardens and plenty of help – or time to spend – in the garden. Most of us, however, find this type of border impracticable, and the herbaceous border has largely evolved into the mixed border, in which shrubs of varying sizes are used to provide a permanent framework within which herbaceous perennials are planted.

Should I raise herbaceous perennials from seed or buy plants from a garden centre?

Ever-larger sections of seed catalogues are devoted to perennials, and it would appear that, as long as you have a greenhouse and a cold frame, the same results can be achieved for a fraction of the price of buying plants.

The major drawback to raising perennials from seed, however, is that only a limited range of varieties of each type of plant is available, and often the varieties available are not the best. This is because many types of plant simply do not come true from seed and must be propagated by cuttings. Moreover, most of the perennials offered as seed are hybrid mixtures, which will give rise to plants in a range of colours and of varying quality. If you want to know exactly how your plants will appear when they are mature, you should buy them as plants rather than raising them from seed.

The second major advantage to buying herbaceous perennials as plants is the time taken to flower. Few seed-raised plants can be guaranteed to flower in the first season, whereas most of those bought as plants will do so. Remember, too, that once you have paid for a single initial plant, you will always be able to increase your stock in years to come by taking cuttings or by division.

RIGHT: Many plants simply can't be raised from seed so buying them 'ready-made' is your only option.

What advantages do herbaceous perennials have over other types of plant?

The term 'herbaceous perennial' encompasses plants that have a wide range of flower sizes, shapes, colours and flowering times and that are able to continue to produce blooms year after year without having to be replaced each spring. Herbaceous perennials thus score over annuals, which last for a season, over shrubs, which flower for much shorter periods, and over bulbs, which have some above-ground show for only a short period of the year.

Against these merits must be set the facts that some herbaceous perennials need staking or other support, and that they also require lifting and dividing every few years. In addition, their winter appeal, while greater than that of annuals, is less than that of shrubs.

LEFT: Border irises are among the few perennials that require little or no staking.

I would like to create a blue and yellow border. What perennials do you suggest?

Blue and yellow has become a popular colour combination in recent years, although it is important to find true colours for the best effect and to avoid purples and oranges. The following are my top suggestions for some easy-to-grow summer-flowering perennials to start your collection. Bear in mind that other varieties of the species recommended may have differently coloured flowers:

BLUE
- *Campanula* 'E.K. Toogood'
- *Delphinium* (many)
- *Echinops bannaticus* 'Blue Globe'
- *Echinops ritro* 'Veitch's Blue'
- *Eryngium bourgatii* 'Oxford Blue'
- *Geranium wallichianum* 'Buxton's Variety' (syn. *G.* 'Buxton's Blue')
- *Geranium* 'Johnson's Blue'
- *Iris* (many border cultivars)
- *Linum narbonense* 'Heavenly Blue'
- *Veronica austriaca* subsp. *teucrium* 'Crater Lake Blue'

YELLOW
- *Achillea tomentosa* 'Aurea'
- *Buphthalmum salicifolium*
- *Geum* 'Lady Stratheden'
- *Helianthus* 'Capenoch Star'
- *Hemerocallis* (several)
- *Inula hookeri*
- *Inula magnifica*
- *Iris* (several border cultivars)
- *Kniphofia* 'Little Maid'
- *Ligularia przewalskii*
- *Ligularia stenocephala*
- *Oenothera fruticosa* 'Fyrverkeri'
- *Rudbeckia* 'Goldquelle'

Should I divide and plant herbaceous perennials in autumn or spring?

Deciding when to divide and plant herbaceous perennials will depend partly on where you live, partly on how busy you are and partly on the types of perennial you grow. If you buy herbaceous perennials in containers from a nursery or garden centre, you can fairly safely plant them at any time of the year, provided that the ground is neither frozen nor waterlogged. Removing an established plant from the open ground is a different matter, however, for it will experience extensive root disturbance, and this should be avoided when a plant is in full growth. Autumn is generally the best and most convenient time. Exceptions to this rule are perennials such as peonies and hellebores, which resent disturbance, usually because they have thick, fleshy roots; it is better to move these in spring, shortly before growth recommences, especially in colder areas.

LEFT: Yellow and blue is one of the most satisfying and soothing of colour combinations.

I have heard someone recommend 'herbaceous clematis'. What are they?

Most clematis are climbers, but there is a small number of excellent, lower-growing herbaceous types, which mix well with other plants in the border. They are becoming increasingly popular, and several new cultivars are available. The commonest you will find are *Clematis heracleifolia* and its cultivars, including 'Côte d'Azur', with pale blue flowers, and 'Wyevale', which bears blue, hyacinth-like flowers in late summer on stems 60–120cm (2–4ft) long. Also available is *C. integrifolia*, which grows to about 75cm (30in) and bears blue, bell-shaped flowers in midsummer; 'Pastel Blue' has light blue flowers, and 'Rosea' has pretty, deep pink flowers. *C. recta*, the most vigorous herbaceous species, bears masses of small, white, sweet-scented flowers on rather floppy stems to 1.5m (5ft) long.

Give herbaceous clematis similar conditions to the climbing types and, preferably, alkaline soil, but do not try to stake them. This is never really successful, and they look much better when they are allowed to scramble over and through other, bushy plants. Prune by removing all top growth in early spring.

My pampas grass is enormous but lacks flowers. Why?

It is likely that you have a plant that was initially raised from seed rather than being a named cultivar that was propagated by division. This is a rather common phenomenon with many other types of plant and is an additional reason why raising perennials from seed may not always have the advantages that may at first seem obvious (see page 17). You might like to replace your plant with *Cortaderia selloana* 'Sunningdale Silver', which will grow 3m (10ft) high) or, if space is limited, *C. selloana* 'Pumila', which reaches only about 1.5m (5ft) and produces masses of flower plumes.

LEFT: *Cortaderia selloana* 'Pumila' is an excellent shorter- growing pampas grass.

Is it possible to grow herbaceous perennials satisfactorily in a poor, shady site?

Shade is certainly not a problem for many fine perennials; poor soil definitely is, however, and poor soil, especially when it is combined with shade, should always be improved with compost, leafmould and fertilizer.

The following herbaceous perennials are fairly tolerant of shade, and some will even tolerate dry conditions. *Asarum europaeum*, an excellent ground-cover plant, is usually evergreen, but it may shed its leaves in a very cold winter. Bear in mind that astilbes will not tolerate dry conditions at all.

ABOVE: The lovely *Geranium himalayense* is typical of the many perennials that really do need mulching well.

	LIGHT SHADE	MODERATE SHADE	DRY SOIL
Aconitum hemsleyanum (aconite)	yes	yes	no
Aconitum napellus (monkshood)	yes	yes	no
Alchemilla mollis (lady's mantle)	yes	no	yes
Aruncus dioicus (syn. *A. sylvester*; goatsbeard)	yes	no	no
Asarum europaeum (wild ginger)	yes	yes	no
Astilbe hybrids	yes	no	no
Astrantia spp. (masterwort)	yes	yes	no
Bergenia spp. (elephant's ears)	yes	yes	yes
Cimicifuga racemosa (black snake root)	yes	no	no
Digitalis spp. (foxglove)	yes	yes	yes
Euphorbia amygdaloides var. robbiae	yes	yes	yes
Geranium phaeum (dusky cranesbill)	yes	yes	yes
Helleborus foetidus (stinking hellebore)	yes	yes	yes
Helleborus argutifolius (Corsican hellebore)	yes	yes	yes
Lamium galeobdolon (yellow archangel)	yes	no	yes
Lamium maculatum (dead nettle)	yes	no	yes
Omphalodes cappadocica (navelwort)	yes	yes	no
Tiarella cordifolia (foam flower)	yes	yes	no

How important is mulching for herbaceous perennials?

The short answer is 'very important'. Even species that are tolerant of fairly dry conditions will benefit from the improved moisture-retaining properties that mulching imparts to soil. Bear in mind, however, that a surface mulch will maintain the soil in its existing condition. If you mulch dry soil, it will remain dry, so always apply a mulch after it has rained or after you have given the soil a thorough soaking.

A spring mulch will help to conserve the moisture in the soil throughout the coming summer. An autumn mulch has the rather different benefit of protecting the crowns of perennials from penetrating winter cold. The best overall mulching material is leafmould; the next best is compost.

Can you suggest some perennials that will grow well on a heavy, clay soil?

The problems with clay soil – at least, as far as plants are concerned – are that it retains water and it is cold, which means that it can become almost waterlogged in winter and will warm up very slowly in the spring. It does have some great advantages once it has been cultivated because it holds plant nutrients and releases them slowly to satisfy the plants' needs. In order to capitalize on these attributes, however, the coldness and the extreme water-retentiveness must be corrected, and there is no better way of achieving this than to introduce organic matter, such as garden compost, well-rotted farmyard manure, spent mushroom compost or almost anything that comes to hand (or fork).

Many plants grow naturally in clay soils and many will do so in your garden. The following are some of the best and most reliable:

- *Acanthus* (bear's breeches)
- *Alchemilla* (lady's mantle)
- *Bergenia* (elephant's ears)
- *Caltha* (marsh marigold)
- *Epimedium* (barrenwort)
- *Euphorbia amygdaloides* var. *robbiae*
- *Helleborus* (hellebore)
- *Hosta* cvs.
- *Primula* (some, including candelabra primulas)
- *Trachystemon orientalis* (eastern borage)

ABOVE: Hostas are very versatile plants and are particularly good in heavier soils.

STAKING PERENNIALS
1 Push twigs into the soil around a plant for effective support.
2 A plant will grow up around a proprietary ring stake to hide it.
3 L-shaped interlocking wires can be joined together to accommodate quite large plants.

 **1**
 **2**
 **3**

Is there an easy way of avoiding the problem of having to stake and tie in herbaceous perennials every year?

The simplest way to overcome the problem is to select varieties with stouter, stiffer stems or to select some of the dwarf forms that are now available. Some type of support is essential, however, if you want to grow many of the best, traditional, tall herbaceous perennials, including delphiniums and hollyhocks. The usual method is to place a cane, preferably green and at least two-thirds of the eventual height of the plant, behind the upright stem and to tie in the plant as it grows. An alternative labour-saving and less visually intrusive method for lower-growing plants, such as some types of *Centaurea* (knapweed), is to place from three to five canes around a group of stems and to tie twine around the whole, rather than staking each stem individually.

Some plants, including *Paeonia* cultivars (peonies), produce really dense clumps of massed stems, and inserting twigs around the clump before the flowering stems have elongated will provide effective support and eliminate the need for tying in. A supply of suitable twigs is not easily found, however, and in recent years, several proprietary supports have come on to the market. These consist of metal rings, tripod structures on legs or L-shaped interlocking wires, sometimes with adjustable heights and diameters. They are simple to use and effective but not cheap. They are, however, reusable.

LEFT: *Aster thomsonii* 'Nanus' is a very reliable low-growing Michaelmas daisy which remains mildew free.

My Michaelmas daisies are always badly affected by mildew. How can I avoid this?

All Michaelmas daisies are forms of perennial species of *Aster*, and most of the older varieties belong to *Aster novi-belgii*, a species that is particularly susceptible to powdery mildew. Some of the taller-growing cultivars are fairly reliable, including 'Coombe Rosemary' (double, purple), 'Freda Ballard' (semi-double, red) and 'Patricia Ballard' (semi-double, pink). The best lower-growing cultivars include 'Little Pink Beauty' (semi-double, pink), 'Jenny' (double, purple) and 'Snowsprite' (white).

A better approach, however, is to select cultivars of quite different species. There are some very beautiful pink and red forms of *Aster novae-angliae* (New England aster), particularly 'Andenken an Alma Pötschke' and 'Harrington's Pink', both of which are widely available. Perhaps best of all, however, are the plants derived from *Aster amellus*; the hybrid form known as *A. frikartii* has the classic Michaelmas daisy lavender colour and is a superb plant. *A. amellus* 'Rosa Erfüllung' has pale pink flowers, and 'Veilchenkönigin' has violet-coloured flowers. Finally, if you prefer a lower-growing plant, look out for the outstanding *A. thomsonii* 'Nanus', which has lavender-coloured flowers and grows to about 45cm (18in) high.

Even when you have selected a good variety, remember that mildew is encouraged by warm, dry conditions, and so paying attention to regular watering and the generous use of mulches around the plants will help to maintain a moist environment.

If you want to continue to grow cultivars of *A. novi-belgii*, you will almost certainly have to use a fungicide. Remove and burn any infected leaves as soon as you see them to prevent the problem spreading.

Which perennials can I use to provide colour after spring-flowering bulbs in a southwest-facing border beneath two huge trees?

Some of the shade-tolerant plants mentioned on page 20 will be successful in this type of site, but the problem here is less one of lack of light than of thin, impoverished soil, and it is essential to do as much as you can to improve its quality. Use leafmould or compost lightly dressed with a general fertilizer, such as fish, blood and bone, and fork it lightly into the surface as frequently as you can.

Because it will be difficult for large plants to develop a deep root system under big trees, you should concentrate on low-growing types. In addition to *Asarum* (wild ginger), *Bergenia* (elephant's ears), *Lamium* (dead nettle) and *Omphalodes* (navelwort), you could also try *Astrantia* (masterwort), *Calamintha* (calamint), *Geranium macrorrhizum*, *Heuchera* (coral flower), x *Heucherella*, *Phuopsis stylosa*, *Pulmonaria* (lungwort) and ornamental forms of *Ranunculus ficaria* (lesser celandine) such as 'Brazen Hussy'. All these plants, however, need moist soil, so adding humus must be a priority.

How can perennials be encouraged to give a good show quickly?

Any plant will respond more quickly if care is taken with soil preparation and planting. This is especially true if the soil in your garden is too wet, too dry, too heavy or too light, and taking steps to improve the quality of the soil by digging in well-rotted garden compost will always pay dividends. If you do not like to see bare soil in your borders, however, you can hurry things along by planting groups of three or five plants rather than isolated individuals or by planting more closely than is recommended on labels and in catalogues. You can always thin out and remove individual plants later on, when the plants begin to look overcrowded, and you may regard it as a small price to pay for not having to look at bare patches of soil for several years. An alternative – and less expensive – solution to the problem of bare ground is to sow annuals around the perennials.

ABOVE: *Kniphofia uvaria* 'Nobilis' is among those perennials that take time to establish so are best planted in groups of three or five.

Black spots have appeared on the leaves and stems of my Christmas rose. What is causing this and is it serious?

This is a common problem with *Helleborus niger* (Christmas rose) and related species, although it has nothing to do with the black spot that afflicts real roses. When it occurs on the leaves it may just be disfiguring, but when it is on the stems it can lead to rotting at soil level. Remove and destroy all infected foliage. If the attack is severe, apply Bordeaux mixture or another copper-containing fungicide, spraying two or three times at monthly intervals, beginning in autumn and continuing until the new growth ceases.

ABOVE: Leaf spot is common on several different types of *Helleborus*. This is *Helleborus argutifolius*.

How should I treat my herbaceous perennials in autumn?

Applying a mulch of leafmould or compost will help to protect the crown from penetrating winter frost and will also keep the soil moist and encourage root development. Some gardeners advocate cutting back all dead flower stems, which both looks neat and avoids the danger of accidentally damaging young shoots when you tidy up the border in spring. Other gardeners prefer to leave seedheads until the birds have had their fill, and they look very attractive with frost and snow on them. The leaves of evergreen perennials such as kniphofias (red-hot pokers) should be tied lightly together to protect the crowns.

RIGHT: Leaving the dead stems and seedheads over winter provides food for the birds and can look extremely beautiful.

What is the best way to grow hardy ferns?

Ferns are among the most fascinating, beautiful and rewarding of plants. Most require shady, damp sites, although a few can tolerate drier and more exposed situations. Most ferns also prefer neutral to acidic soil, but a few, such as *Polypodium*, require alkaline conditions. I have devoted a damp, shaded corner of my own garden in which little else would grow to a collection of ferns, but I also dot individual ferns among other plants, in woodland, at the back of shrubberies and in the shadier parts of mixed borders. Small species, such as *Adiantum* spp. (maidenhair fern), fill crevices in damp walls, and ferns also combine well with other large-leaved foliage plants, such as hostas, in moist, shaded borders or near water. Deciduous ferns die down with the first frosts, but leaving the old fronds in place over winter will provide protection for the crowns. Look out for the many species and cultivars in the following genera:

- *Adiantum* (maidenhair fern)
- *Asplenium* (spleenwort)
- *Blechnum* (hard fern)
- *Cystopteris* (bladder fern)
- *Dryopteris* (buckler fern)
- *Matteuccia* (ostrich fern)
- *Polypodium* (common polypody)
- *Polystichum* (holly fern, shield fern)

ABOVE: *Matteuccia struthiopteris* is easy to grow but can be invasive in confined areas.

Why do my dahlias look spindly and have small flowers? What is the best way to grow them?

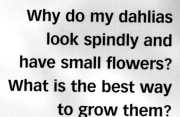

The key to success with dahlias is to start with strong, healthy stock and then to appreciate that large, lush leaves and big flowers need adequate watering and feeding. Dahlias thrive in a sunny position with a deep, moist but freely draining soil. The addition of well-rotted manure or compost to the soil in autumn will benefit dahlias by improving the moisture retentiveness of a free-draining soil or by opening up a heavy one, and it will provide a modest supply of nutrients. If the soil is light enough not to need further extensive cultivation before planting in spring, a dressing of bonemeal should be applied with the manure in autumn. Routine liquid feeding in summer will also help, not only in producing good plants during the season but also in making sure that sound tubers are built up for the following year.

Climbers

RIGHT: The large-flowered hybrid clematis, like 'Elsa Späth' are very prone to wilt disease.

My clematis grow for a couple of years and then die. Why?

Buying a clematis
Clematis, especially the species clematis, do not like root disturbance, and when you are buying a new plant, avoid bare-root plants. Look for clematis with dark green foliage and with the roots just appearing from the base of the pot. The surface of the soil of any plant that has been in its pot for too long will be covered with moss; avoid these plants. Although container-grown specimens can be planted at any time of the year, avoid buying in summer unless you are sure that you will be able to water your plants regularly and thoroughly. Remember, too, that clematis will do best with a cool, moist and rich root run, but in ground that will not be waterlogged in winter.

The problem is almost certainly a mysterious disease called clematis wilt. It is mysterious because no one is quite sure what causes it, although it is probably partly fungal. Most of the large-flowered hybrid cultivars are susceptible to attack, although species clematis are much less likely to be affected. Cut back the plant to ground level or below, drench the surrounding soil with a systemic fungicide, such as carbendazim, and wait and see. Quite often the plant recovers and is restored to perfect health.

When a plant dies back repeatedly, however, it must be dug out and disposed of. Remove the soil to a depth of about 30cm (12in) and the same distance across, and replace with fresh soil from another part of the garden. Then, when you are planting the new clematis, bury it much deeper that you would normally – at least 15cm (6in) below the soil mark on the stem – to encourage the formation of stem roots, which appear to be less susceptible to infection.

ABOVE: Many types of climbing rose look their best when trained over an arch or pergola.

Is it better to grow climbers against a wall or a more natural support?

Your decision will depend partly on the type of climber and partly on the type of wall. With non-self-clinging climbers, the more the plant resembles the wild form, the more appropriate it will look on a natural support. *Lonicera* (honeysuckle) is a good example, and they often look more attractive when they are grown over trees, big shrubs or even old fences than when they are trained on a trellis against a house wall. On the other hand, a more 'artificial-looking' flower, such as *Clematis* 'Nelly Moser', is probably at its most appealing when it is grown on, or close to, a building.

Self-clinging climbers – that is, plants such as *Hedera* spp. (ivy), *Parthenocissus quinquefolia* (Virginia creeper) or *P. tricuspidata* (Boston ivy), which produce aerial roots or clinging tendrils – are different. They are best kept away from trees and allowed to cling to a wall, provided that the wall is well constructed of sound bricks or stone and strong mortar.

I thought clematis were supposed to be easy to strike from cuttings. Where am I going wrong?

Some clematis are easy to strike from cuttings, but there are two important factors to remember, and overlooking these is why many people fail. First, although species clematis are comparatively easy to strike, the large-flowered hybrids are much more difficult. Second, clematis are unusual in that the piece of stem that is to form the cutting must be cut between two nodes (the bumps where buds occur and leaves arise), not just below the node and bud as with most other plants. Push the cutting into the compost so that the node itself is just above the surface of the compost.

ABOVE: *Clematis montana* looks wonderful growing as it does naturally, through a tree.

Will allowing a clematis to grow through its branches damage a tree?

The tree will not be harmed unless it is very young and the clematis is a very vigorous one, such as *Clematis montana*. In their natural habit many clematis grow through trees, and the small-flowered types in particular look much more attractive when they are grown in this way.

ABOVE: Persuading a rose to flower from top to bottom is all in the training.

My climbing rose persistently flowers at the top only. What can I do to persuade it to flower at the base as well?

This is probably the commonest of all problems with all flowering climbers and roses are the commonest culprits. The plant flowers at the top because of something called apical dominance – that is, the bud at the end of a shoot produces a chemical that inhibits buds further down from developing. The solution is simple. Instead of allowing the shoots to grow vertically against a wall, pull them down to a horizontal position, tie them in to the support and cut off as much other growth as necessary to fit the allotted space. This will disrupt the apical dominance, and buds will burst along the length of each shoot.

I would like to cover a south-facing wall with climbers. Can I grow some of them in containers?

Like almost every other type of plant, climbers can be grown successfully in containers. In some respects they are well suited to being grown in pots because they are naturally fairly tolerant of the dry conditions that occur at the base of walls and hedges and that are often found in containers. *Clematis alpina* and *C. macropetala* will adapt to being grown in pots, and it is even possible to grow wisteria in a container, provided that it is pruned hard back regularly and the container is large.

Some climbers, however, especially roses, have deep tap roots rather than an extensive fibrous root system, and do not adapt well to container growing. If you are anxious to grow roses, try some of the miniature climbing roses, which grow to about 2m (6ft) high – 'Jean Lajoie' (double, lavender-pink), 'Little Rambler' (double, pale pink) and 'Captain Scarlet' (semi-double, bright red), for example, will grow happily in pots. Remember, too, that all plants that are grown in containers in the long term need a nutrient-rich compost, such as John Innes No. 3, as well as regular top-dressing and feeding and, above all, watering.

Top-dressing

Plants that are grown in containers eventually use up all the nutrients in the compost. There will come a time when the plant has been re-potted into the largest available container, and when this happens it is important regularly to renew the top 2–5cm (1–2in) of soil. In spring, therefore, carefully remove the old compost from the top, making sure that you do not damage any of the delicate roots near the surface as you work. Fill the gap with new compost. It is a good idea to mix some slow-release fertilizer granules into the new compost, so that the nutrients are washed down the container as you water. You should also apply a mulch, such as gravel or bark chippings, to aid moisture retention.

What is a pillar rose and how do I grow one?

First, find a pillar; second, plant a rose against it. The pillar is usually a tree trunk or a stout post about 2m (6ft) high and securely anchored in position. The rose can be a medium sized, fairly upright-growing shrub rose or a compact, non-vigorous climber. The word 'Pillar' in the rose's name is no guarantee that it will be suitable, however – 'Paul's Lemon Pillar' and 'American Pillar', for example, are too tall. The rose should be planted to one side of the pillar and its shoots trained around it in a spiral. It is then pruned much as any conventional climbing rose by cutting back the side shoots to within about 5cm (2in) of the main stems each year. The effect is very attractive because the rose should flower uniformly from top to bottom. The following roses make excellent pillar plants:

- ❀ 'Aloha' – double, pink
- ❀ 'Dublin Bay' – double, rich red
- ❀ 'Königin von Dänemark' – double, soft pink
- ❀ 'Meg' – semi-double, yellow-pink
- ❀ 'Scabrosa' – single, deep pink
- ❀ 'Tuscany Superb' – semi-double, dark red

ABOVE: Don't be misled by this picture; 'American Pillar' is too vigorous to use as a pillar rose.

ABOVE: *Viburnum* x *burkwoodii* isn't a climber but when pruned carefully and trained against a wall, it looks like one.

Does growing climbers mean I shall have to do plenty of pruning?

Not necessarily. Remember that climbers are no more than long, thin shrubs that need extra support, so they shouldn't really need pruning any more frequently than their free-standing counterparts. When climbers are allowed to grow in a semi-natural fashion – over old buildings, through the branches of trees, on large pergolas and so on – they may need almost no pruning. Climbers do require extra attention when they have to be kept neatly trained against a more formal support, such as a small trellis attached to a wall. Even here, however, the plant will almost always require slightly harder or more severe pruning, rather than more frequent pruning.

Do self-clinging climbers really damage brickwork?

Self-clinging climbers – that is, plants that ascend by means of aerial roots or adhesive tendrils – will damage the surface against which they are growing only if that surface is already defective. Well-pointed brickwork and good mortar will not be damaged. Crumbly bricks and mortar (especially lime mortar) will eventually be pulled apart, however. In effect, therefore, climbers such as *Hedera* (ivy) and *Parthenocissus* spp. (Virginia creeper) should not be grown on an old, unsound wall although they will be perfectly safe on a modern one. Having said that, however, I have some old, free-standing walls in my own garden that are covered in ivy, and it is the ivy that stops the walls from falling down.

RIGHT: *Hedera colchica* is too vigorous to be grown against a house wall, as it is here, and will soon damage old bricks and mortar.

LEFT: *Passiflora caerulea* is the only reliably hardy passion flower for British gardens.

I love passion flowers. Are they sufficiently hardy to grow in my garden?

There are many wonderful species of passion flower, and it is true that most are too tender to grow outdoors. There are, however, two forms that will survive winter temperatures of –5°C (23°F). A good deal of the above-ground growth will be damaged by frost in hard winters, but these plants do, in any case, benefit from hard pruning in the spring when the dead shoots can be cut away. The two reliable forms are the fantastically exotic-looking, blue-flowered *Passiflora caerulea* and the white-flowered form 'Constance Elliott'.

Although some perennial climbers can be raised from seed, they are, for the reasons outlined on page 17, usually inferior to named varieties bought as plants. Nevertheless, there are many splendid annual climbers that can be raised readily from seed and that will provide wonderful blooms during the summer months. The following are among the best:

Annual climbers with attractive flowers
* *Caiophora lateritia* – in mild areas this can be grown as a biennial or perennial
* *Cobaea scandens* (cup-and-saucer plant, cathedral bells)
* *Codonopsis* spp. (climbing bellflower)
* *Eccremocarpus scaber* (Chilean glory flower)
* *Ipomoea tricolor* (morning glory)
* *Lathyrus odoratus* (sweet pea)
* *Maurandella antirrhiniflora* (climbing snapdragon)
* *Rhodochiton* spp.
* *Thunbergia alata* (black-eyed Susan)
* *Tropaeolum majus* (nasturtium)

Annual climbers with attractive foliage
* *Tropaeolum majus* 'Alaska'
* *Tropaeolum majus* 'Jewel of Africa'

Annual climbers with attractive fruit
* *Caiophora lateritia*
* *Cucurbita* (gourds)

BELOW: *Trachelospermum jasminoides* is a most exquisite, fragrant climber for slightly milder gardens.

There are very few climbers with both attributes, and, in truth, there are only a few evergreen climbers of any sort that can be grown outside in areas with cold winters; most are simply not sufficiently hardy to survive without their foliage become unattractively browned. *Hedera* (ivy) is probably the toughest evergreen climber, but even that will be damaged in very cold weather – and, of course, its flowers are hardly exciting. You might, therefore, prefer to plant *Clematis armandii*, which is much hardier than many people imagine and has gloriously perfumed white flowers in spring. For slightly milder areas or more sheltered walls, *Trachelospermum jasminoides* (star jasmine, confederate jasmine) is a delightful choice. Another plant that is much hardier that many people realize and is well worth trying is *Hydrangea serratifolia* (syn. *H. integerrima*), the evergreen climbing hydrangea which is not to be confused with the much commoner, deciduous *H. anomala* subsp. *petiolaris*.

LEFT: *Tropaeolum speciosum* dies back in winter but is stunningly lovely every summer.

I have heard that there are perennial nasturtiums. What can you tell me about them?

Nasturtiums belong to the genus *Tropaeolum*, and the popular half-hardy annuals mentioned on page 31 are forms of *Tropaeolum majus*. The yellow-flowered *T. peregrinum* (Canary creeper) is also a half-hardy annual. There are, however, two widely grown perennials in this genus, of which the more often seen is *T. speciosum* (flame creeper), which bears bright red flowers from mid- to late summer and sometimes bright blue fruits in autumn. It will reach a height of about 3m (10ft), and although it is native to Chile it really is hardy enough to be grown in cold areas, as its other common name, Scottish flame flower, suggests. It is often grown – and is seen at its best – scrambling through an evergreen shrub or hedge, such as *Taxus* (yew). The above-ground growth should be cut back to soil level in autumn. *T. tuberosum* is rather similar but has bright orange-scarlet flowers and is reliably hardy only in milder areas.

Should climbers be fed differently from other garden plants?

There is no need to use a different type of plant fertilizer, but you should be prepared to apply it more frequently. As already noted (see page 28), climbers tend to grow in dry, often rather impoverished soil at the base of walls or other plants, such as hedges, and they will benefit if extra care is taken in preparing the soil when they are planted through the addition of good compost and bonemeal, and also if they are fed carefully throughout the growing season. Try applying rose fertilizer in spring (when the roses are fed) and again in early summer (also when the roses are fed), with an additional once-a-month treatment with soluble fertilizer throughout the summer.

I would like a climber with really huge leaves. What do you suggest?

Assuming that you want a perennial – given that some annual climbers such as gourds have big leaves – there is really only one choice: the ornamental vine *Vitis coignetiae*. This has stunning leaves, to 30cm (12in) long, which turn a glorious red before dropping in autumn. Remember that the leaves do drop, and raking up the debris is a considerable task each year. *V. coignetiae* is best grown over a structure such as a trellis or pergola because it is not self-clinging and will require considerable support if it is grown against a wall. It will tolerate most soils.

ABOVE: *Vitis coignetiae* not only has huge leaves, it also has exquisite autumn colour.

ABOVE: *Akebia quinata* is a favourite of mine and is unusual for its aroma of chocolate.

Which five climbers do you think have the best fragrance?

So many climbers have good perfume that your choice will really depend on the situation in which you want to grow them and what other plants you have nearby to create an attractive blend of colours. Although they may appear to be rather obvious choices, the following list includes a rose, a honeysuckle and a clematis, all of which are reliable and fragrant. The other two suggestions are more unusual but just as attractive in the right setting:

❀ *Akebia quinata* (chocolate vine) is an unusual semi-evergreen plant, with small, brownish-purple flowers, which have the fragrance of chocolate.

❀ *Clematis montana* 'Elizabeth' is a vigorous plant, bearing masses of pale pink flowers in spring. It has the best fragrance of all the deciduous clematis.

❀ *Lonicera periclymenum* (common honeysuckle, woodbine) is a big plant but has a consistently better fragrance than *L. periclymenum* 'Belgica' (early Dutch honeysuckle).

❀ *Rosa* 'Gloire de Dijon' is an old rose and a bit sparse on foliage, but it has large, double flowers, which are a glorious peach colour.

❀ *Trachelospermum jasminoides* (star jasmine, confederate jasmine) is evergreen and bears small, white flowers; it is self-clinging and hardy in most areas if it is in a sheltered position.

I have just moved into an old house with a grape vine trained into the greenhouse from outside. Why was this done?

This is the best way to plant a grape vine because the roots will benefit from the natural moisture in the soil and from natural rainfall, while the main part of the plant has the advantage of being in the warmth of the greenhouse. In many ways, moisture is the key to growing grapes successfully, for without copious supplies of water the fruits will not swell and ripen satisfactorily. Yet the enormous amount of foliage means that a huge volume of water is lost through evaporation. You should also give your vine a watering can of liquid fertilizer about every three weeks throughout summer. If you are planting a new vine in a greenhouse, this is the best way to grow it, and if you want a trouble-free variety, try *Vitis vinifera* 'Schiava Grossa' ('Black Hamburgh').

BELOW: *Clematis alpina* 'Frances Rivis' is one of the best early season climbers for a north facing aspect.

Can you suggest some climbers for a north-facing wall?

Gardeners often imagine that a north-facing wall poses a problem because of the damage that cold and frost will cause to any plants growing against it. In reality, although it may be cold, frost may be less of a problem because the real damage from frost occurs when frozen plants thaw out quickly. This is more likely to happen on an east-facing wall, where the plants receive the early morning sun, than on a north-facing one. Some of the following plants may not be as hardy as you might imagine, but they don't need to be:

❀ *Clematis alpina* and its forms are none-too vigorous clematis, which produce relatively small but very attractive flowers in the early part of the year; 'Frances Rivis' bears a mass of blue, bell-shaped flowers.

❀ *Hedera helix* 'Buttercup' (ivy) is a lovely old cultivar if you want something that is not too vigorous and that has attractively coloured small leaves; but do bear in mind the comments on page 30 about the risks of growing ivy on old walls.

❀ *Holboellia coriacea* is an evergreen climber, native to China, which will make an unusual subject for a north-facing aspect as long as your garden is not too cold.

❀ *Hydrangea anomala* subsp. *petiolaris* is a self-clinging, deciduous climbing hydrangea, with white flowers (although you should not expect anything as large as the mop-head shrubby hydrangeas).

❀ *Rosa* 'Climbing Ena Harkness' is a strikingly lovely rose, bearing very deep red flowers; it is one of several roses that are fairly tolerant of a north-facing aspect but I have singled it out because I have grown it on a rather dark wall.

Can I rejuvenate an old, gnarled and rather rotten wisteria?

Yes: wisterias are almost indestructible. Give it a hard pruning in winter, leaving 5cm (2in) side-shoot stubs on the main branches. Prune it again in late summer by cutting the new green side-shoots back to 25cm (10cm). Cut out any rotten parts, cutting well into the healthy wood.

ABOVE: Wisterias are almost indestructible; and invariably look much older than they really are.

I have been given a kiwi vine. Why are there two plants in the same pot?

The reason for this odd arrangement is that most forms of *Actinidia deliciosa* (kiwi fruit or vine, Chinese gooseberry) are unisexual, and two separate plants are needed for successful fertilization and fruit. Nurseries find it convenient to plant the two in the same container, and they should be planted together but trained in opposite directions. They will bear fruit only if they are grown in a greenhouse or in a sheltered garden.

If you are growing kiwi fruit for the first time, bear in mind that they are very vigorous and you must give them adequate space. They should be pruned in the same way as a grape vine.

Hedges, fences & boundaries

Which makes the best garden boundary, a fence, a wall or a hedge?

For most gardeners cost is the main factor when it comes to deciding which type of garden boundary to have, and this is followed by effectiveness and speed of obtaining the desired effect. Unfortunately, aesthetic and other considerations take a lower priority. Wherever possible, however, the boundary should match both the property and the garden – brick walls in towns but possibly not in the country, for instance. I make no secret of the fact that I prefer hedges but concede that you can't have them instantly. The chart below should help you to make the most practical choice.

FENCE Relatively inexpensive

* Quick to erect
* Modern paints offer versatility
* Provides good support for climbing plants
* Can be monotonous, although some modern (if more costly) fences may be more attractive
* Fairly unstable in high winds (perforated types, such as wattle, are better in windy sites)
* Will deteriorate after about 10 years and then need to be replaced

HEDGE Moderately expensive

* Attractive when mature
* Provides cover for wildlife but also for overwintering pests
* Slow to establish
* Offers only limited support for climbing plants
* Requires constant maintenance
* Deciduous types offer less privacy and cover in winter

WALL Very expensive

* Comparatively quick to erect
* Robust if not indestructible
* Can be attractive (depending on design)
* Provides good support for climbing plants
* Unless gaps are provided, wind eddies may result in an accumulation of debris

TOP: Wicker panels make an attractive fence.
MIDDLE: Hedges needn't be boring; this is an escallonia hedge in full flower.
BOTTOM: Walls can be softened by careful planting.

My neighbour's 2-metre (6-ft) high fence casts a shadow over part of the garden for most of the day. What plants would brighten things up?

Suggesting bright plants for shady places is always difficult because relatively few produce colourful flowers in these conditions. The majority of flowers that are produced in shade tend to be green, white or other less obvious colours. The following plants have brightly coloured flowers, and I have found them particularly reliable:

- *Dicentra spectabilis* (bleeding heart) – a low-growing perennial with deep pink flowers
- *Impatiens* (busy Lizzie) – annuals that are available in a range of shades of red and pink and in white
- *Lysimachia* (loosestrife) – perennials with yellow flowers
- Rhododendron – shrubs in a wide range of red, pink, purple and yellow and white
- *Viola labradorica* (Labrador violet) – a small, low-growing perennial with purple flowers
- *Waldsteinia ternata* – a low-growing perennial with yellow flowers

If you have acid soil you might also try *Photinia villosa* and *Pieris*, which have vivid red young shoots; other shrubs, such as *Gaultheria* spp., have brightly and variously coloured fruits.

Wind protection

If you are uncertain how high a boundary you need to protect your garden, remember that a hedge, fence or other barrier will lessen the strength of the wind for a distance on the leeward side equal to approximately ten times its height. A boundary 2m (6ft) tall, therefore, will have a protective effect on the garden and the plants grown in it for about 12m (36ft) downwind.

Can you suggest a suitable plant for a low hedge to protect my vegetable plot from north and west winds?

A low hedge can be created with either a vigorous plant that must be cut frequently or a less vigorous plant that will take longer to achieve the desired height. In a relatively mild area and given that this is a vegetable plot, *Rosmarinus officinalis* (rosemary) would be appropriate. In a colder garden I would choose either *Rosa rugosa* or *Crataegus* (hawthorn), although the latter is slower growing.

What is the best way to propagate conifer cuttings from a parent tree to make a wind-break screen?

Conifers are never easy to propagate without special facilities, and the provision of an almost constantly moist atmosphere by means of a mist system is essential. If the parent plant is a cypress – either *Cupressus* or *Chamaecyparis* – you could be in for disappointment. Most conifers do not achieve the right degree of woodiness for cuttings until early winter, mainly because the bulk of the new growth takes place after midsummer and then needs several more months in which to toughen up. However, by all means try taking heeled cuttings (those with a small sliver of wood from the parent stem attached) in early spring and then keep them as moist as possible.

A relatively low-cost alternative is to buy rooted cuttings in bulk from a forest tree nursery. They will be supplied as bare-rooted plants and must be planted promptly, but they will be immeasurably cheaper than the potted plants you will find at a garden centre.

ABOVE: Pyracanthas are classic wall shrubs and obtainable with red, orange or yellow fruits.

Can you suggest a fast-growing plant, needing very little pruning, that I could plant against a 2-metre (6-ft) high fence?

I would plant a pyracantha in such a position. It is certainly a common enough shrub, but it is one that I have come to appreciate more and more as the years go by, both as a wall shrub and as a free-standing specimen or hedge.

Pyracanthas, which are sometimes called firethorns, belong to the rose family, and they have three special attributes: they are evergreen, they have attractive flowers, and they have colourful fruits. The blossom appears in white masses in early summer, and the berries colour the plants from late summer onwards. The real glory is undoubtedly the fruits, which may be red, orange or golden. Rather surprisingly, the three look very pretty when differently coloured varieties are mixed together. I would recommend:

❀ *Pyracantha coccinea* 'Lalandei' (syn. *P.* 'Monrovia') or *P.* 'Watereri' – red berries

❀ *P. rogersiana* – orange berries
❀ *P.* 'Soleil d'Or' – yellow berries

How can I make sure that my hedge grows quickly and thickly?

I am always surprised at how little attention is given to hedges compared with other shrubs, especially as they often have a crucial structural part to play in the garden, and, *en masse*, they cost a great deal of money.

When you are planting a new hedge, always prepare the trench thoroughly. Dig in plenty of organic matter and add a generous application of bonemeal.

To improve the growth of an existing hedge, give an application of a general fertilizer – fish, blood and bone, for example – every spring and then, later in the year, when the soil is moist (use a hosepipe if it is not), give a generous organic mulch. I would guess that there is not one gardener in a thousand who gives their hedge this simple, routine attention, but it will pay dividends many times over.

Can you suggest some ideas for horse- and sheep-proof screening along a long, exposed garden boundary?

Finding plants that are resistant to the attentions of sheep and horses suggests that prickles and thorns are required, and, in theory at least, the scope is considerable – shrub roses, berberis, *Ilex* spp. (holly) and *Crataegus monogyna* (hawthorn), for instance, would all be suitable. Tolerance of an exposed position is exhibited by all these, except perhaps berberis, which will scorch.

Cost, however, is likely to be an important factor for a long boundary, and I think that this will limit the choice to hawthorn. This really has stood the test of time as a farm boundary, and the miles of hawthorn hedging all over the country are testimony to the fact that it is highly tolerant of exposure and also of alkaline conditions.

I want to tackle a large, old beech boundary hedge by cutting it back. Will I kill it?

I would be unhappy about undertaking this work. *Fagus* spp. (beech) will tolerate being cut back into old wood, but not as effectively as, say, *Taxus* spp. (yew). A major problem with beech is that it is prone to a disease called coral spot, which invades through pruning cuts and then spreads down into the living parts of the branch. My advice would be to cut back the hedge by about one-half and work on only one side at a time. Wait to see if there is successful regeneration before taking the process any further.

ABOVE: Beech is a superb hedging plant but should be cut regularly so it doesn't become overgrown.

Which roses do you recommend for use in hedges?

As a group, the tough and disease-resistant rugosa roses surpass all others as informal – that is, not clipped – hedging; these are the roses that are planted on roadsides and on central reservations. For low, informal hedges any low-growing rugosa rose is suitable, also 'Mousseline' (sometimes known as 'Alfred de Dalmas'), 'Portlandica' (syn. 'Duchess of Portland') or 'White Pet'. If you prefer something slightly taller and more modern in style, look out for 'Ballerina' , 'Felicia' or 'F.J. Grootendorst'. For a tall hedge try the well-known old rugosa rose 'Roseraie de l'Haÿ' or modern roses such as 'Nevada', 'Scabrosa' or 'The Queen Elizabeth' among modern ones.

A few roses will tolerate clipping, and the best of these are the sweet briars, like 'Meg Merrilies' and 'Magnifica', or some of the albas, such as *Rosa* x *alba* 'Semiplena' and *R.* x *alba* 'Alba Maxima'.

ABOVE: *Rosa rugosa* varieties such as 'Roseraie de l'Haÿ' make excellent hedges.

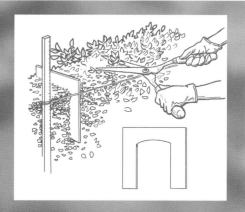

Trimming hedges

Cut the hedge so that it is narrower at the top than at the bottom. To get a smooth, even curve it is worth making a template from hardboard or stiff cardboard, which you can move along the top of the hedge as you work. If you live in an area that regularly suffers prolonged snowfalls, cut the hedge so that it has a pointed top to allow the snow to slide off.

USING A TRIMMING TEMPLATE
It is very easy to make a template to aid your hedge trimming; not many of us can achieve perfect results by eye.

What is the best way to clip my hedge and when is the best time of year to do it?

The timing of hedge clipping is governed by two main considerations: how fast does the hedge grow (and how much more will it grow after it is clipped and before the end of the season) and when do birds finish nesting? In general, you should clip twice: first in early summer, but after birds have fledged and will not be disturbed, and again in mid-autumn, but don't leave it too late or frost will damage the cut shoots.

Electric hedge trimmers are much the best way to clip all but very short hedges. Make sure that you have the necessary protection: goggles, gloves and a circuit breaker. Unless you have a very good eye, use string, attached to canes or posts and set with a spirit level to give a straight line.

BELOW: To my mind, dwarf box has never been surpassed as a plant for dwarf hedging.

Can you recommend a hedge for a seaside garden, where it will be subject to wind and salt spray?

Seaside gardens offer special challenges, and providing a hedge to protect plants from salt and wind is very important. The need for the hedge itself to be tolerant of these conditions places special demands on it, but the fact that many seaside gardens are fairly mild offers some interesting choices.

If the density of the screen is not a consideration and you live in a mild area, *Fuchsia magellanica* is a possible candidate; in a slightly colder garden *Tamarix* spp. (tamarisk) might appeal to you. If you need something more robust, *Escallonia* cultivars are the best choice, followed by the beautiful *Griselinia littoralis*, which is not reliably hardy. In colder areas *Cotoneaster*, *Crataegus* (hawthorn), *Elaeagnus*, *Euonymus japonicus* (Japanese spindle) and *Hippophäe rhamnoides* (sea buckthorn) would be suitable. Conifer hedges will almost always be browned unacceptably.

What are the best species to choose for dwarf hedges similar to those used around herb gardens?

To re-create a traditional herb garden you really need to use a plant that was available when this type of garden was first developed, and for this reason dwarf box, in the form *Buxus sempervirens* 'Suffruticosa', really has no rivals, although it is slow-growing. Another traditional plant is *Santolina chamaecyparissus* (cotton lavender), but it is much less neat and less amenable to being clipped. The other option would be *Rosmarinus officinalis* (rosemary).

My own formal herb garden is attractively edged in dwarf box, around which is a path and then a slightly higher hedge of *Taxus* (yew).

Trees & shrubs

Can you recommend some trees for a small garden?

ABOVE: *Amelanchier lamarckii* has long been my favourite small tree and is lovely all year round.

In limited space a tree that produces attractive blossom must be a prime choice, although it is important that there is also some other attractive characteristic for the remaining weeks and months of the year. The following suggestions, therefore, include trees that produce flowers but that also have another feature to recommend them.

You may be surprised that there are no flowering cherries in this list. This is because they have become rather prone to disease in recent years and there are, in any case, many better things. The heights shown are those to be expected on good soils after 10 and 20 years of growth.

* *Amelanchier lamarckii* has delicate winter twigs, small white flowers in spring, soft green foliage in summer and rich autumn leaf colours and fruit; 4m (13ft), 6m (20ft).
* *Cercis siliquastrum* (Judas tree) bears bright pink, broom-like flowers in late spring; 3m (10ft), 5m (16ft).
* *Eucryphia nymansensis* 'Nymansay' is an evergreen, which needs shelter from cold wind; it has large, single, white flowers in late summer; 5m (16ft), 9m (30ft).
* *Genista aetnensis* (Mount Etna broom) has

green shoots and masses of yellow flowers in late summer; 5m (16ft), 7m (23ft).
* *Laburnum* x *watereri* 'Vossii' (Voss's laburnum) produces masses of very long, pendulous flowerheads; 7m (23ft), 8m (26ft).
* *Magnolia* x *soulangeana* has large, white, tulip-shaped flowers, with varying amounts of purple; 2m (6ft), 3m (10ft).
* *Malus* 'John Downie' (flowering crab) has white flowers; 5m (16ft), 8m (26ft); *M.* 'Profusion' has deep red flowers and coppery red leaves; 3m (10ft), 5m (16ft).

Do you think that garden trees need staking?

In general, trees should be staked until they are about 5m (16ft) tall. In my experience the short stakes that have recently become popular are often inadequate, and I would strongly recommend that tall stakes, about 2m (6ft) high, be used. Remember to make sure that you use a purpose-made, belt-style tree tie.

LEFT: Evidence enough for my lack of faith in short stakes for trees.

Is it better to propagate trees from cuttings or from seeds or is neither method worthwhile?

True species are best propagated from seed, but it is a slow business. The seeds should be stratified – that is, they should be placed on a layer of horticultural sand in a shallow terracotta pot, covered with another layer of sand and then left outdoors through the winter. The cold weather will break the dormancy of the seeds, which should then germinate, a few at a time, in the spring. Hardwood cuttings taken in winter are perfectly satisfactory, but it is less easy to achieve success with them unless you have specialist propagating facilities.

A third and very important method for the many varieties that do not come true from seed is grafting, and many of the ornamental trees that you buy from nurseries will have been grafted. This is not something that most gardeners will want to attempt, however.

How large a tree can be planted with a fair chance that it will survive?

A large tree, grown under normal conditions and simply dug up and transplanted to a new site, is unlikely to survive. Trees are, however, now being raised, either in containers or in the open ground in special soil and with special root preparation, solely for the purpose of being transplanted to give 'instant' landscaping effect. If this is what you want and can afford, be sure to obtain the trees from an experienced specialist nursery; make sure, too, that you have help with the planting. Most big conifers transplant much less satisfactorily than most broad-leaved trees.

Can you suggest a range of fairly small trees with interesting bark?

Attractive bark is one of the less often appreciated features of trees. When you are selecting from the suggestions listed below, bear two things in mind: first, the effect of bark is greatest in winter, partly because there are no other distracting features but also because the colours may intensify at that time of year; and second, the effects become increasingly apparent as a tree ages.

* *Abies squamata* (silver fir)
* *Acer griseum* (paper-bark maple)
* *Acer davidii, A. grosseri* var. *hersii* and other snake-bark maples
* *Betula utilis* (Himalayan birch), *B. utilis* var. *jacquemontii* and related birches
* *Cornus officinalis* (dogwood)
* *Eucalyptus* spp. (gum)
* *Prunus* spp. (ornamental cherry), especially *P. serrula*
* *Salix* spp. (willow)
* *Taxodium* spp. (swamp cypress)
* *Thuja* spp. (arborvitae)

ABOVE: The snake-bark maples have some of the loveliest of all bark patterns.

RIGHT: Knopper galls on acorns have become extremely common but oak trees don't appear to have suffered in consequence.

Why are the leaves of my flowering cherry tree curled and infested with insects?

The fact that ornamental cherries are susceptible to so many problems is the main reason I no longer recommend them (see page 42), and people who already have established trees in their gardens must expect to see these infestations by a species of aphid called the cherry blackfly. Like most aphids, these insects prefer the soft young foliage at the shoot tips, and before the end of the season the terminal leaves have often dried and shrivelled. Do not spray during the growing season, but if the tree is not too large, applying a spray of tar oil in winter, when the tree is dormant and leafless, should have some effect. The insects survive the winter as eggs on the bark, and the spray should eliminate many of them.

The acorns from our local oak trees are distorted. Does this mean that the trees themselves are diseased?

Oaks are among the most durable of trees, and a little distortion of the acorns will not harm them unduly. The problem has become extremely common since it was first found in southern England in 1960, and many people have expressed concern. The acorns have been attacked by a species of insect called the acorn cup gall wasp, and the symptoms have acquired the name of knopper galls. They are among the numerous fascinating things you will find on oak trees, which are host to more species of insect than any other British tree.

ABOVE: This is bad planting; the tree is too close to the house and is also a weeping willow which can cause problems for both drains and foundations.

How close to my house can I safely plant a tree?

It is wise to consider a tree's ultimate size and its position in relation to the house before any tree is planted anywhere in the garden. Many, many problems would have been avoided if previous garden-owners had given the matter a little thought. It is an important aspect of gardening planning, principally because root growth can cause damage to the house's foundations, while the exclusion of light from the house (and neighbours) is another, important consideration.

The question is not entirely straightforward, however, because the likelihood of damage depends on the type of tree and the type of soil. Heavy, clay soils tend to shrink as they dry, and because a large tree acts as a pump, drawing out water, the greatest stresses occur in such conditions. In general, whatever type of soil you have in your garden, it is better not to plant a tree closer to the house than a distance equal to one and a half times its ultimate height. Trees with a high water intake – *Salix* spp. (willow) and *Populus* spp. (poplar) are much the most important of these – should not be planted closer than three times their ultimate height. These distances could be increased by 50 per cent on very heavy soils.

LEFT: *Parrotia persica* is a fairly large tree but one with beautiful autumn foliage.

What is the best tree for autumn colour?

Maples are many gardeners' automatic choice for autumn colour, although they are seldom as dramatic in Britain as in North America. The suggestions here include trees that are reliable and appealing during the remainder of the year – it is all too easy to choose a tree that looks wonderful for two weeks and forget that you will have to live with it for the remaining fifty. The heights given are those that can be expected on good soils after 10 and 20 years:

❁ *Acer griseum* (paper-bark maple) – 3m (10ft), 5m (16ft)

❁ *Acer palmatum* 'Osakazuki' (Japanese maple) – 2m (6ft), 5m (16ft)

❁ *Acer platanoides* 'Schwedleri' (Norway maple) – 8m (26ft), 13m (43ft)

❁ *Acer rubrum* (red maple) – 8m (26ft), 12m (40ft)

❁ *Amelanchier lamarckii* – 6m (20ft), 9m (30ft)

❁ *Betula ermanii* 'Grayswood Hill' (syn. *B. costata*) – 8m (26ft), 12m (40ft)

❁ *Betula utilis* var. *jacquemontii* – 8m (26ft), 12m (40ft)

❁ *Crataegus persimilis* 'Prunifolia' (syn. *C.* x *prunifolia*) – 3m (10ft), 5m (16ft)

❁ *Liquidambar styraciflua* (sweet gum) – 5m (16ft), 12m (40ft)

❁ *Liriodendron tulipifera* (tulip tree) – 8m (26ft), 16m (53ft)

❁ *Parrotia persica* (Persian ironwood) – 4m (13ft), 7m (23ft)

❁ *Prunus sargentii* (Sargent cherry) – 5m (16ft), 9m (30ft)

❁ *Sorbus commixta* – 6m (20ft), 9m (30ft)

❁ *Sorbus* 'Joseph Rock' – 6m (20ft), 12m (40ft)

❁ *Stewartia pseudocamellia* – 5m (16ft), 9m (30ft)

My ornamental cherry 'Kanzan' is now 20 years old and not flowering well. Is it just old age?

The Japanese ornamental cherry *Prunus* 'Kanzan' was one of the most widely planted flowering trees in gardens and street plantings during the third quarter of the 20th century. It was used on countless suburban housing developments, and gardeners followed suit. 'Kanzan' and its relatives are extremely distinctive trees, bearing masses of double, vivid pink blossom, but it is now much less widely planted, for two main reasons. First, shocking pink was very much a colour of its time and it has fallen from favour. Second, the problem identified in the question. Ornamental trees have limited lives, and 'Kanzan' comes to the end of its allotted span after about 30 years. This process has been accelerated by outbreaks of disease, which are manifest by a general decline in vigour, a lack of flowers and a gradual dying back of the branches. No one seems sure of the cause, although it appears to be a bacterial attack of some kind. It is apparent that the trees do not recover, and I would advise any gardener facing this problem to replace the 'Kanzan' with something different. Look at the suggestions listed on page 42.

ABOVE: Recent outbreaks of disease mean that the assertive pink blossom of *Prunus* 'Kanzan' is now being seen rather less.

BELOW: You will rarely find a holly without signs of leaf miner attack but it seems to cause no harm to the tree.

What has caused the disfiguring yellow patches on the leaves of my holly, 'J.C. van Tol'?

Hollies are valuable garden trees, not least because they are susceptible to few pests and diseases, but this is one of the problems that does arise. The disfiguring patches are the result of attack by the holly leaf miner, a species of fly whose larvae tunnel within the leaf tissues and cause the characteristic damage. There are comparable leaf miners on many other types of plant, and they rarely cause serious harm. If they are seriously disfiguring, pull off the affected leaves and destroy them.

Ilex aquifolium 'J.C. van Tol' is a particularly good and reliable holly, with almost spineless leaves and plenty of red berries.

What has caused a mysterious split in the trunk of my *Acer* 'Brilliantissimum'?

Acer pseudoplatanus 'Brilliantissimum' is the only cultivar of sycamore worth growing in gardens. The parent is a dreadful tree, but this form has lovely, pinkish foliage in spring although it later darkens to green. Like many species of *Acer*, however, the main trunk is prone to splitting for reasons that no one fully understands. Sometimes bacterial attack can be responsible, but in these cases there is usually a coloured slime oozing from the split. Do nothing; just wait and see. Trees often recover, and the wound will heal. If you are ever in any doubt, contact a qualified tree surgeon to assess the damage.

LEFT: *Acer pseudoplatanus* 'Brilliantissimum' is a fine garden tree and in such marked contrast to its wild parent.

BELOW: I would never have tried growing a tulip tree in a container but this shows that with care and attention, it can be done.

Can a tree be grown in a large tub?

All plants can be grown in tubs, and it may simply be a matter of finding a container large enough for a tree. Check the ultimate height and growth rate of your chosen species first, however. It is not a good idea to plant very fast-growing species in tubs because re-potting a tree is no easy matter. It is also wise not to choose species such as *Salix* (willow) that require large amounts of water – the compost in the tub will inevitably dry out frequently and continual watering, twice a day in hot weather, will become something of a chore. Always use a very high quality, nutrient-rich potting compost, such as John Innes No. 3. You will also need to apply a general fertilizer once or twice a year. The following hardy trees will adapt readily to container conditions:

* *Acer palmatum* Dissectum Atropurpureum Group
* *Cupressus macrocarpa* (Monterey cypress)
* *Juniperus scopulorum* 'Skyrocket'
* *Laurus nobilis* (sweet bay)
* *Taxus baccata* (yew)

The new leaves and blossom of my hawthorn turned brown, and I noticed masses of tiny caterpillars. What is wrong with it?

Leaves turning brown on *Crataegus* (hawthorn) should always be investigated carefully because the symptom could be the result of an attack by the bacterial disease fireblight. Together with *Pyrus* spp. (pears) and certain other woody members of the rose family, such as *Pyracantha* (firethorn), hawthorn is susceptible to this serious problem. If fireblight is found, the affected plant should be pruned hard back, well past the damaged branches, or the plant should be dug up and burned.

In this instance, however, close examination has paid dividends because the caterpillars betray the fact that this is an attack by the hawthorn webber moth. A number of species of caterpillar have the habit of producing cobweb-like webbing to protect themselves, and they are not easy to control because sprays tend to be thrown off by the webs. Carefully cut away and destroy badly affected shoots, and if the problem persists apply an insecticide such as permethrin.

ABOVE: The so-called copper beech will always be a big tree as dwarfing rootstocks are not available but there is a narrow, fastigiate variety called 'Dawyck Purple'.

Is it possible to obtain trees such as beech and oak on some form of dwarfing rootstock?

Unfortunately, *Fagus* spp. (beech) and *Quercus* spp. (oak) are not available on dwarfing or, to give them their correct name, growth-limiting rootstocks. These have been bred for use with fruit trees, where they exert a size-regulating effect on any variety grafted on to them. The greatest successes have been with apples, followed to a much lesser extent by pears and plums. The only non-fruit trees that benefit are those like ornamental crab-apples that are very closely related to the fruiting species.

There is another way in which trees such as beech and oak might be grown in a limited space, however. This is by using varieties that are limited not in overall size or even in height, but in width. There are so-called fastigiate forms, which have a relatively narrow, columnar habit of growth, and they are found in a considerable number of tree species, including beech and oak. *Fagus sylvatica* 'Dawyck' (Dawyck beech) grows to about 7m (23ft) across, and *F. sylvatica* 'Dawyck Purple' to about 5m (15ft) across, while *Quercus robur* 'Fastigiata Koster' is a columnar tree that will grow to 28m (92ft) high.

Is it really possible to choose completely disease-resistant rose varieties?

Sadly, no one can tell how long resistance to a given pest or disease will last. The roses with the most long-lasting resistance have been the shrubs and climbers derived from *Rosa rugosa*, which are called rugosa varieties, but if you choose from the most recently introduced cultivars you will fare pretty well because they will have been thoroughly tested before release and should be effective for a good many years. The biggest difficulty is likely to arise with yellow-flowered roses, which almost invariably have a higher than average susceptibility to black spot.

ABOVE: Few rose varieties are reliably resistant to all diseases but modern varieties are generally the most dependable.

Is there any way to prevent suckers growing from the roots of my roses?

Choosing new plants from among the new cultivars that are available now will reduce, if not wholly eliminate, the problem. This is because the rootstock on to which modern flowering roses are grafted will probably be a form of the European wild rose species *Rosa coriifolia*, popularly called 'Laxa'. In the past, *Rosa canina* (dog rose) was used as a rootstock, and this was much more prone to produce suckers.

No matter what type of rose you have, suckers should always be removed because they rob the rose of nutrients. Carefully remove the soil from around the rose so that the point of origin on the root can be seen and then tear the sucker away. Wear stout gloves for this task. If the sucker is cut off, more suckers are likely to arise. If you take cuttings from your roses, the resultant plants will, of course, be growing on their own roots, so any 'suckers' will be of the same variety.

Is it better to have evergreen or deciduous shrubs?

In an ideal world, gardens would contain a mixture of both types of shrub, but that avoids the issue. Forced to choose between them, I would opt for deciduous shrubs but would select carefully to make sure that there was a range of varieties offering some appeal in the form of flowers, bark, buds or fruit during the winter months when the foliage has gone. With their year-round foliage, evergreens would seem to offer reliable, 12-month appeal, but the appearance is unchanging and, for that reason, less attractive.

REMOVING A SUCKER
If suckers are left in place, the appearance and performance of the variety will gradually diminish, as the rootstock from which suckers emerge is invariably more vigorous. Suckers should be pulled rather than cut away to discourage more suckers from arising.

ABOVE: Any shrub trained against a wall is technically a wall shrub but with naturally spreading varieties, the amount of pruning required will be considerable.

What exactly is a wall shrub?

A wall shrub is nothing more or less than a shrub growing against a wall. Of late, the expression has been used a good deal in gardening literature, when it generally refers to a rather restricted range of plants – *Pyracantha* (firethorn), *Chaenomeles* (flowering quince), *Jasminum* (jasmine) and so on – which can readily be pruned so that they assume a general two-dimensional form. In reality, however, a huge number of shrubs will grow very well against a wall and will benefit from the added warmth and protection that the wall offers. Such plants as *Carpenteria californica, Ceanothus, Ribes speciosum* and many other choice species can be grown in this way when they would be unlikely to survive in the open garden.

Remember that any shrub grown against a wall will benefit from extra care being taken in soil preparation and extra attention being given to regular feeding and watering because the conditions at the base of a wall are usually dry and impoverished.

My flowering currant grows in the shade, and for the last two years it has been covered with a black film. What is the problem?

The problem is called, not surprisingly, sooty mould, and it arises when dark types of mould fungi are attracted to, and grow on, a sticky, sugary substance called honeydew. This is, in turn, produced by sap-sucking insects such as aphids and whitefly. That it is often a problem on plants growing in shade has nothing to do with the shade itself but with the fact that the shade is caused by a large tree. *Tilia* spp. (lime) and *Betula* spp. (birch) are particularly notorious for attracting aphids, which drip the honeydew on to any plants growing under the trees. There is nothing directly that can be done, although deciduous plants, which acquire a fresh set of leaves each spring, will be less likely to suffer than evergreens, on which the mould can build up over a long period.

ABOVE: Black sooty mould growth is common on plants, like this beech hedge, that are infested with aphids or other sap-sucking pests.

Do shrubs need feeding?

If you want to obtain the very best from the shrubs in your garden, you should certainly feed them. It is a straightforward process: feed them twice a year, once in early spring and once in early summer. If their appeal is mainly as flowering varieties, use a proprietary rose fertilizer; if they are grown mainly for their foliage, use fish, blood and bone.

Which shrubs would give autumn colour in a small garden?

We tend to think of autumn colour more in terms of trees than of shrubs (see page 46), but dramatic effects can be achieved in gardens that are too small even for one tree if some of the wide range of attractive shrubs are included. The following are especially reliable and garden-worthy.

- *Acer* (maple): although most acers are really trees, some are certainly small and others so slow growing that they rarely reach more than shrub size in many gardens. There are several forms of *A. palmatum*, especially *A. palmatum* Dissectum Atropurpureum Group, which provide excellent autumn colour.
- *Berberis* (barberry): most berberis colour well, but *B. thunbergii* is the best of all, and many of its forms, such as 'Atropurpurea Nana', 'Dart's Red Lady' and the variegated 'Rose Glow', have purple foliage in summer, which later turns fiery red.
- *Ceratostigma willmottianum*: invaluable for its late, clear blue flowers, this shrub also has foliage that in most years turns a rich red.
- *Cornus* (dogwood): the dwarf dogwoods, especially *C. florida* (flowering dogwood), have leaves that turn red, purple and orange in autumn.
- *Cotinus* (smoke bush): this is perhaps the best of all shrubs for autumn colour, and one of the very best is *C. coggygria* 'Royal Purple'.
- *Cotoneaster*: many provide good autumn colour, but there are few reds more vivid than that of *C. horizontalis*.
- *Rhus* (sumach): although these plants are dramatic in autumn, they have little appeal in winter.
- *Rosa* (rose): the yellows of the rugosa roses are best, and *R. rugosa* itself bears large red or orange-red hips.
- *Stephanandra*: the leaves of *S. incisa* 'Crispa' turn a vivid golden colour.
- *Viburnum*: two deciduous species which have excellent autumn colours are *V. carlesii* and *V. opulus* (guelder rose).

ABOVE: Most types of mop-head hydrangeas will produce blue flowers naturally only on acidic soils.

I would love to be able to grow blue hydrangeas but mine always turn pink. Is there anything I can do?

The mop-head types of hydrangea have pink flowers when grown on alkaline soils and blue flowers when grown on acidic soils with a pH of less than about 5.5. You can encourage blue flowers to develop if your soil is fairly neutral by watering in a substance called 'bluing powder', which is obtainable from garden centres.

What is the ideal soil for growing shrubs?

ABOVE: With an acidic soil, you can grow rhododendrons to perfection; but if you haven't got acidic soil, you should choose other shrubs instead.

The fact that there are shrubs for almost every type of soil is one of their great merits. No matter where your garden is situated, there will be shrubs that will thrive in it. But choice is important. While there are shrubs adapted to every possible soil, there are many that will not do well in soil that is less that optimal for them. In the lists below, therefore, I've indicated five good and easy shrubs that are ideal for acidic soils (but nowhere else), five for alkaline soils (and less satisfactory anywhere else); and five that will tolerate both extremes. Many other shrub species will tolerate a wide range of soils within the extremes.

Shrubs that require acidic soil
- Camellia
- Erica (heath)
- Photinia beauverdiana and P. serratifolia
- Pieris
- Rhododendron/Azalea

Shrubs that require alkaline soil
- Caragana spp. (Siberian pea tree)
- Caryopteris x clandonensis and C. incana
- Chimonanthus praecox (wintersweet)
- Cistus spp. (rock rose)
- Deutzia spp.

Shrubs that tolerate both alkaline and acidic soils
- Berberis vulgaris
- Ilex spp. (holly)
- Ligustrum spp. (privet)
- Sambucus racemosa (cut-leaved elder)
- Viburnum opulus (guelder rose)

Testing your soil

Soil-testing kits are sold in many garden centres, and they are not expensive. Although your soil type may be quite obvious from the wonderfully glossy leaves of a calcifuge camellia or the colourful blooms of the alkaline-tolerant *Gomphrena globosa*, pH levels can vary within even a fairly small garden. Follow the instructions which come with the kit and take samples from several places. The small outlay on the kit may save you from buying expensive plants that simply will not thrive in your garden.

Some of the branches on my red rhododendron have produced purple flowers. Is this plant a freak and what can I do about it?

You do not have a freak in your garden – the purple flowers are simply an indication that the variety has been grafted on to a rootstock of the purple-flowered and widely naturalized species *Rhododendron ponticum*. This is done by nurseries because the flowering variety does not have a very vigorous root system. Just as with roses and any other plant that produces suckers in this way, you should use strong gloves and tear the sucker away from the roots. If you leave it, *Rhododendron ponticum*, which is a very vigorous plant, will gradually take over.

LEFT: Azalea gall is a common and disfiguring problem, especially on evergreen varieties and often causes concern.

ABOVE: The vigorous, naturalized species *Rhododendron ponticum* is often used as a rootstock for other varieties.

What has caused the small galls on my azaleas?

The growths you have noticed are the common symptom of rhododendron gall disease, which occurs most commonly on indoor pot azaleas. Small, irregular swellings arise on leaves, buds or flowers. At first these are often reddish, but later they become chalky-white as a covering of spores develops. Flowering is reduced, and general growth and vigour may suffer.

Snip off the individual galls, preferably before they turn white and shower spores on to healthy flowers and foliage. Do not take cuttings from affected plants.

Just how effective are ground-cover shrubs?

These shrubs are fairly effective when it comes to covering the ground and hiding bare soil, but they vary in their effectiveness at suppressing weeds, which is, in theory, one of the most appealing attributes of this type of plant. This is nothing to do with whether they are deciduous or evergreen, because a good cover of leaves, even if it is present only from spring to autumn, will fairly reliably suppress weed growth. The variation in their effectiveness as weed suppressers is more to do with the openness of their texture. Ground-cover roses are particularly poor at weed suppression because the cover is less than complete, and, of course, their thorns make hand weeding among them extremely difficult. The following ground-cover shrubs are especially good at weed suppression:

- *Calluna vulgaris* (heather, ling) – on acidic soils only
- *Euonymus fortunei* cvs.
- *Hedera helix* cvs. (ivy)
- *Salix repens* var. *argentea* (creeping willow)
- *Stephanandra incisa* 'Crispa'

Alpines

What is the best way to grow alpines in the garden?

ABOVE: A stone (or replica stone) trough is the perfect way to grow alpines in a small garden.

I would suggest that the best way to grow alpine plants is in a container. Although, like most people, I used to grow alpines in a 'rock garden', this is not ideal because it seldom looks either quite right or sufficiently natural. A good rock garden should appear to be a natural rocky outcrop; and in most modern gardens, this simply could never happen.

A much better home for alpines is a trough. A real stone trough would be perfect, but the price of second-hand troughs has made this an impossible ideal for most gardeners, and a perfectly acceptable alternative is an artificial replica (see page 60).

Real enthusiasts for alpine species tend to grow individual plants in single clay pots, which are kept in an alpine house, where they can be protected from wet weather in winter.

Why do alpines always seem to have gravel around them?

Gravel – in practice, sharp, angular stone chippings are better than smooth gravel – is placed around alpine plants for three main reasons, all of which are important. First, it prevents soil from being splashed on to the foliage and flowers. Such marks are, of course, unsightly, but more important is the fact that the gravel prevents the spores of potentially damaging moulds and other fungi in the soil from being splashed on to the plants. Second, the gravel helps to maintain the moisture in the compost at a fairly uniform level. Third, it looks very attractive and helps to set off the beauty of the plants themselves.

Do check that alpine plants that require acidic compost are mulched with stone chippings or grit that are 'lime-free'; similarly, plants that prefer alkaline compost should not be surrounded by acidic grit.

RIGHT: Gravel or stone chippings not only display alpines to perfection, they also minimize rotting.

How can I create an alpine lawn?

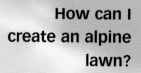

Creating an alpine lawn is a wonderful challenge for a lover of alpine plants. It is an emulation of one of those areas of low-growing turf that occur at high altitude, not only in the European Alps, of course, but in other mountain ranges, too.

Choose an area of very well-drained soil in as sunny a position as possible. The bulk of the ground area should be taken up with very low-growing, carpeting and mat-forming plants. There are many to choose from, but one that I find useful in many situations where modest ground cover is required is *Acaena*, a genus from New Zealand, which is characterized by wiry stems and small, spiky, burr-like flowerheads. Among other easy-to-grow plants that can be used to form the basic carpet in these conditions are thymes, preferably species such as *Thymus pseudolanuginosus*, alpine phlox, *Antennaria* (cat's ears) and dwarf species of *Achillea* among many others. Within this turf should be placed discrete clumps of such plants as the tufted *Festuca glauca* (blue fescue), *Dianthus deltoides* (maiden pink), large numbers of saxifrages, of course, and *Corydalis cava*. Then plant dwarf bulbs, which will peep up through the carpet in spring and summer – scillas, crocuses, miniature narcissi, dwarf alliums and fritillaries would be very effective.

Why do my mossy saxifrages always turn brown in the middle?

This is a very common problem, and one that has afflicted plants in my own garden. I am not sure that the reason is the same in every case, but it certainly seems to be the paler coloured, faster growing, softer foliaged saxifrages that are most susceptible. Moisture accumulating in the centre is probably one factor, and this may be compounded either by frost damage (or, more specifically, rapid thawing) or by hot sun. The problem is lessened by giving a little more shelter to these slightly more 'delicate' plants (delicate being, of course, a relative term with alpines).

There is a mass of bindweed entrenched in my rock garden. How can I eradicate it without major structural engineering?

This is a job for a small hand sprayer and some weedkiller containing the translocated chemical glyphosate. Choose a warm, sunny day in summer and use pieces of cardboard to shield your plants while you direct the spray on to the bindweed. Weedkillers containing glyphosate are also sold in a gel formulation for 'painting' on the weed's leaves, but this does not appear to be as effective as the spray. You will need to repeat the treatment two or three times, choosing warm, dry days for every application. The bindweed will gradually turn yellow and die away. The glyphosate will damage any plants with which it comes into contact, but it does not persist in the soil.

Using weedkillers

Before you use any chemicals in the garden, read the manufacturer's instructions carefully, especially those relating to quantity and timing. Make sure, too, that you are wearing appropriate protective clothing if necessary.

LEFT: *Oxalis adenophylla* was the first alpine plant I ever bought and it has been a favourite ever since.

Can you suggest some easy-to-grow alpines for a beginner?

It is probably true to say that most of the alpines you will find at your local garden centre will be fairly easy to grow. The more difficult types tend to be sold by specialist nurseries, which should indicate any special cultural requirements and likely problems in their catalogue descriptions. Nevertheless, do bear in mind that some of the plants sold as 'alpines' in garden centres are really very aggressive and will soon take over; check with the list opposite before you buy. Among the easiest to grow and most interesting alpines are:

- *Armeria maritima* (sea thrift)
- *Aubrieta* x *cultorum* cvs., especially double-flowered
- *Erodium reichardii* (syn. *E. chamedryoides*; stork's bill)
- *Oxalis adenophylla* (sorrel)
- *Potentilla eriocarpa* (cinquefoil)
- *Primula* x *pubescens* cvs.
- *Ranunculus ficaria* 'Collarette' (double celandine)
- *Saponaria* x *olivana* (soapwort)
- *Silene schafta* (campion, catchfly)
- *Thymus* 'Doone Valley'

ABOVE: *Campanula portenschlagiana* is a very attractive ground cover plant; but not one for limited space.

Every time I buy some alpines, at least one of them seems to want to take over the entire garden. What can I do to prevent this?

Why are there no annual alpines?

There are a few true annual alpines but only a few, simply because the alpine summer is too short to give annual plants time to germinate, produce a seedling, grow to flowering size and set seed again. There is nothing to stop you planting small annuals in your alpine beds, of course, although one practical reason why annual alpines are not especially popular with most alpine gardeners is that the sowing and subsequent removal of the plants disturbs the perennial species. Moreover, the fast-growing annuals can soon swamp the entire bed to the detriment of everything else.

Planting in any confined area runs a risk of one plant becoming over-dominant, and it is as true of alpine beds as it is of small garden pools: one aggressive plant in what is largely a planting of slow-growing species can soon take over. Some of the alpines you should avoid unless you have masses of room are listed below, but do check all alpines for their ultimate size before you plant, and if one plant does threaten to become a nuisance, don't hesitate to pull it out. An alpine bed is almost always a fairly small area, and regular attention is needed to make sure that a balance is retained.

❀ *Acaena novae-zelandiae* (syn. *A. anserinifolia*; New Zealand burr)
❀ *Arabis alpina* subsp. *caucasica* (syn. *A. albida*; rock cress)
❀ *Campanula portenschlagiana* (syn. *C. muralis*; Dalmatian bellflower); *C. poscharskyana*
❀ *Cerastium tomentosum* (snow-in-summer)
❀ *Frankenia thymifolia*
❀ *Saxifraga* (some; many mossy saxifrages are very vigorous)
❀ *Sedum acre* (biting stonecrop); *S. anglicum*

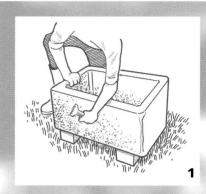

MAKING A REPLICA STONE TROUGH

1 Cover the surface of an old glazed sink with a durable, rough substance, such as the filler used for car bodywork repair. This will give purchase to the hypertufa (replica stone material).

2 Make the replica stone mixture by mixing one volume of sharp sand, one of cement and two of peat with water. The mixture should have the consistency of thick porridge. Paste this over the surface of the sink.

3 Once the mixture is hard, the trough may be planted up in the usual way. The rough surface will soon become colonized with moss and lichens and will almost indistinguishable from the real thing.

What is the easiest way to make a replica stone trough?

BELOW: All plants of *Salix* 'Boydii' are descended from a remarkable little natural hybrid found growing wild in Scotland.

The material that is used is known as hypertufa, and the prohibitive cost of real stone troughs and other containers has made it an effective and attractive alternative. The ingredients (by volume) are one part sharp sand, one part cement and two parts sphagnum peat or similar organic matter. The dry materials should be mixed with water until they assume the consistency of thick, rather stiff porridge. This can be used to coat almost any type of framework, and it is even possible to make statues and similar sculptures by using wire-netting formers, which are coated with the stiff mixture. The most valuable use of hypertufa, however, is in transforming old sinks into replica troughs.

Because the mixture will not adhere to a shiny surface, the exterior surface and top edges should be scored or coated with an adhesive to give some purchase. The materials sold for repairing car bodywork are ideal. The hypertufa can then be coated over the outside of the sink and the top edges. Once it is dry, the hypertufa should be 'painted' occasionally with a weak mixture of milk and cow manure, which will encourage the growth of lichen, algae and moss, which will further enhance its appearance.

If you do not have an old sink or if you would like to have several troughs, make two wooden, topless boxes, one about 5cm (2in) smaller in all directions than the other. Paint the inside surfaces of the larger box and the outside surface of the smaller box with oil so that they can be easily removed. Cut five pieces of wire mesh to fit into the bottom and side gaps between the two boxes. Cut a piece of tube to make a drainage hole in the bottom of the trough, then coat the base of the larger box with hypertufa to a depth of about 2.5cm (1in). Lay a piece of wire mesh on the hypertufa and add another layer so that the hypertufa is about 5cm (2in) deep. Check that the tube is free of hypertufa. Insert the smaller box into the larger one and fill in the gaps all round, placing pieces of mesh along each side about half-way through the hypertufa layer. Leave to set for at least a week before removing the wooden boxes, then coat with milk or yoghurt.

Can you suggest some alpines that are suitable for planting between paving?

Almost any mat-forming alpine will establish itself in the cracks between paving, but not all will last long if the paving is walked on, for many will simply be crushed to death. Among the best that are tolerant of human feet are thymes, but you must remember to choose the true, low creeping varieties and not the bushy forms. The native wild thyme, *Thymus vulgaris*, is satisfactory, but the best is the woolly-leaved and free-flowering *T. pseudolanuginosus*.

The most unexpected, but one of the most successful, plants for paving is *Mentha requienii* (syn. *M. corsica*; Corsican mint), which has minute leaves and even smaller flowers. It will not tolerate heavy traffic, but if you give it a slightly damp area, it will spread with wonderful abandon.

Among the best species for planting where people will not trample them are the tiny blue-flowered *Pratia pedunculata* – *P. pedunculata* 'County Park' has deep blue flowers – and the little white-flowered *Oxalis magellanica*. Also suitable in these conditions are the white form of the native ivy-leaved toadflax, *Cymbalaria muralis* 'Pallidior', and the fern-leaved *Leptinella squalida*.

ABOVE: *Pratia pedunculata* is one of the best plants for planting between paving.

How can I prolong the flowering period of my alpine plants through the summer?

It is widely believed that alpines are really plants for the spring, and it is certainly true that this is when most of them produce their flowers, because in their natural habitat they have to make use of the short period after the snows melt. There are some lovely species to prolong the season, however, and the easiest way to find them is to visit a local nursery or garden centre at regular intervals and buy whatever is in flower. The following are summer-flowering plants from my own collection to give you some ideas:

- *Arabis alpina* subsp. *caucasica* (syn. *A. albida*; rock cress) – as noted on page 59, this can be too vigorous for a small area
- *Armeria maritima* (sea thrift)
- *Aster alpinus*
- *Campanula cochleariifolia* (fairies' thimbles); *C. waldsteiniana*
- *Dianthus erinaceus*; *D. microlepis*
- *Dodecatheon* spp. (shooting stars)
- *Gentiana sino-ornata* (gentian)
- *Geranium cinereum*
- *Globularia cordifolia* (globe daisy)
- *Leontopodium alpinum* (edelweiss)
- *Linum perenne* (perennial flax)
- *Lithodora diffusa* (syn. *Lithospermum diffusum*)
- *Rhodohypoxis baurii*
- *Silene acaulis* (moss campion); *S. uniflora* (syn. *S. maritima*); *S. schafta*

What is your opinion of an alpine shrubbery and is it a realistic proposition?

In addition to some genuine alpine species, there are dwarf or extremely slow-growing forms of several garden shrubs, and these could be used in the larger rock garden. Among those that I grow successfully are:

- *Betula nana* (dwarf birch)
- *Cytisus* 'Cottage' (broom)
- *Genista sagittalis* (broom)
- *Hebe* 'Emerald Green'
- *Hypericum coris* (St John's wort)
- *Potentilla aurea* (cinquefoil)
- *Salix* 'Boydii'; *Salix lanata* (woolly willow)

Vegetables

How can I incorporate attractive and well-flavoured vegetables into an ornamental garden to save both space and time?

ABOVE: A mixture of vegetables and flowers not only looks very attractive but may result in healthier produce if the flowers attract beneficial insects.

You must choose your vegetables carefully. You will never convince anyone that a Brussels sprout plant is pretty, and it is always going to take up a great deal of space for a very long time. There are, however, several attractive, relatively short-term crops that will take up little space and will taste especially good when they are home-grown, and these are appropriate for including with ornamental plants. Try growing carrots, courgettes (bush varieties), cucumbers (bush varieties), dwarf beans, endives, lettuces and radishes, as well as the 'salad leaves', such as rocket, land cress and lamb's lettuce (corn salad).

Why are some vegetables transplanted from seed beds whereas others are sown directly?

The chief reason for transplanting vegetables is that some types grow much more quickly than others. If plants such as cabbages, Brussels sprouts and cauliflowers were sown directly in their growing positions they would occupy the ground for an unreasonably long period of time. With some crops, such as cauliflowers, transplanting makes it possible for the plants to be grown in a cold frame or other protected environment to give them a head-start. With tender plants, such as tomatoes, the option means that the plants can be grown under cover and placed outside only after the danger of frost has passed. Some plants, of course, cannot tolerate the root disturbance that transplanting entails – most root vegetables, such as carrots and parsnips, cannot be transplanted, for example – and even cauliflowers are usually grown in containers rather than as bare-rooted plants to avoid checking their growth.

ABOVE: Brussels sprouts are usually transplanted as they take up plenty of room and grow slowly.

How important do you really think rotation is in the vegetable garden?

Rotation is moderately important, but almost certainly not as vital as is often claimed. It is simply a process by which vegetables of the same or a related type are not grown on the same piece of land in two or more consecutive years. In the most widely applied system, the three-course rotation, they are grown on the same land for one year in three. The advantages claimed for the system are that the soil's nutrients are used to the full, that pests and diseases have time to die away and that the soil is thoroughly cultivated. The first advantage – that the soil's nutrients are fully used – is partly true, but annual applications of fertilizer will make up for any shortfall. The second advantage – that pests and diseases die away – is true for potato eelworm but not much else. The third advantage – that the land is thoroughly dug over – is probably correct.

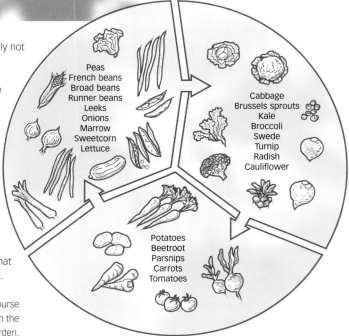

Peas
French beans
Broad beans
Runner beans
Leeks
Onions
Marrow
Sweetcorn
Lettuce

Cabbage
Brussels sprouts
Kale
Broccoli
Swede
Turnip
Radish
Cauliflower

Potatoes
Beetroot
Parsnips
Carrots
Tomatoes

RIGHT: Three-course crop rotation in the vegetable garden.

LEFT: Club root is one of the depressing sights that a vegetable gardener can come across.

Is it possible to control clubroot on my brassicas?

Clubroot causes plants to be discoloured and stunted, and the foliage will wilt. The name derives from the way the roots of affected plants become swollen and distorted. It affects not just brassicas, but also ornamental plants, such as wallflowers and stocks. It is caused by a microscopic soil-inhabiting fungus.

Unfortunately, once the spores of the fungus are in your soil there is little you can do, which is why I urge anyone growing brassicas to raise their own transplants and so avoid the risk of bringing the disease into their garden on the roots of 'imported' plants. If your garden soil is contaminated with clubroot, it will be contaminated more or less forever – the spores of the fungus will remain viable for at least 20 years, perhaps longer – so the best advice is to allocate one area of your vegetable plot to brassicas only (forget about rotation) and apply lime to elevate the soil pH to just over 7 because the disease is worse in acidic, badly drained soils. Raise your plants in individual pots of compost and plant them out in the pot ball. It will not, sadly, be worth growing turnips or swedes, spring greens and possibly even cabbages of any sort, but cauliflowers, broccoli and similar 'high value' crops will make the effort worth while.

I've heard that shallots should be planted on the shortest day of the year. Is this correct?

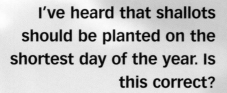

Traditionally, gardeners would plant shallots on the shortest day of the year, and then they would harvest them on the longest day. Now, with the seasons tending to start earlier and finish rather later, most gardeners plant shallots in early spring and harvest them in the second half of summer. Even this is really successful only because shallots are routinely planted as small bulbs, called sets, rather than being sown as seed. This gives them a flying start, and although some shallot varieties can now be obtained as seed, I can see no advantage in this, apart, possibly, from the cost.

Green manure
Nitrogen-rich plants such as clover, rape and mustard can be grown as green manures. The crop is dug into the ground to improve the soil's fertility. While they are growing, the plants provide ground cover and also, in winter, may stop nutrients being washed out of the soil.

I'm entering a giant-marrow-growing competition. How can I make sure I win?

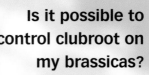

Here is my fail-safe recipe for successful marrows:

* Select a trailing rather than a bush variety; I suggest 'Long White Trailing' or 'Long Green Trailing'.
* Give the plant a long growing season; sow the seed in April indoors and then put out the transplants under cloches until the danger of frost has passed.
* Plant the plant on top of a compost heap to provide both warmth and moisture; marrows come from the humid tropics.
* Apply a liquid feed once a week.
* Remove all but two of the female flowers (those with small swellings just behind the petals); have a plant with male flowers nearby and pollinate the females by picking a male flower and dusting it into them.
* Give water, water and more water.
* Keep an eye out for slugs and combat mildew with a systemic fungicide or a sulphur spray.

And all you will need then is a specially strengthened wheelbarrow to carry the marrow away in triumph.

Can I successfully produce lettuce crops all year round?

This is an achievable aim, but you will need a greenhouse and a deep pocket to pay for extra heating. Here is a possible timetable:

* Summer and early autumn crops: raise young plants in a greenhouse for transplanting outdoors in spring and/or sow in growing positions from spring to summer, using cloches for the earliest sowings. For a successional crop all summer, sow a new row as the seedlings emerge in the previous row.
* Early winter crops: sow in growing positions in summer and cover with cloches from early autumn.

* Christmas and New Year crops (which will be costly): sow or plant in the border or in growing bags in a frost-free greenhouse or (less satisfactorily) outdoors under cloches.
* Early spring crops: sow in growing positions in late summer under cloches or in a cold frame

Always check that the variety you are growing is appropriate for the time of year.

ABOVE: Lettuce is a most versatile plant, in its appearance and cropping period.

ABOVE: Exaggerated claims have been made for the pest-controlling benefits of *Tagetes patula* but flowers of many kinds will attract insects to the kitchen garden.

I want to start an organic vegetable plot. How should I go about it?

All you need do is adhere to generally accepted principles about the way that the plants are fed and the ways that pests and diseases are controlled – that is, you should stop using chemicals to kill pests and combat diseases and rely on organic composts to add nutrients to the ground. You might also want to consider introducing biological controls into your greenhouse – *Encarsia formosa* wasps to combat whitefly, for example – and growing companion plants: *Tagetes* spp. (marigold), for example, attract hoverflies, which feed on aphids. Many gardeners who decide to follow organic principles experience an initial increase in pest levels, but eventually a balance will develop as birds and other friendly wildlife become established in your garden.

You will need to decide, however, if you want to be strictly organic or what I like to call 'common-sense' organic. If you are going to be strictly organic, you will not use any product that is not of natural plant or animal origin. This would preclude you from using fish, blood and bone as a general fertilizer because although the nitrogen source (dried blood) and the phosphate source (bonemeal) are of animal origin, there is no comparable animal source of potash and so potassium sulphate is used. To be strictly organic, you might also want to enquire into the way the animals were reared from which the dried blood and bonemeal were originally obtained. And you might find it difficult to discover if they had been raised organically. The decision on how far you want your organic doctrine to go is, of course, yours, but I believe that 'common-sense' organic gardening at least is a goal towards which we should all strive.

LEFT: Splitting is very common on many tomato varieties at the height of summer.

My 'Gardener's Delight' tomatoes split and turn mouldy. Why?

This seems to be a feature of 'Gardener's Delight', and my own tomatoes have been affected in the same way. Splitting is a common fault with some of the best-flavoured tomato varieties because they tend to have rather thin skins. The only way to try to minimize the problem is by maintaining as uniform a watering regime as possible. Splitting occurs when a period of relatively slow growth (and relative water shortage), is followed by a period when water suddenly becomes available and growth is more rapid. This causes the fruit to swell and the skin splits. Later in the season *Botrytis* (grey mould) infects the tomatoes through the split.

You might like to try the golden-fruited variety 'Sungold', which is otherwise very similar to 'Gardener's Delight', has a comparably excellent flavour but is, in my experience, slightly less prone to split.

What is the optimum time for sowing tomato seeds in a cold greenhouse?

If they are to be the correct size for planting into their final growing positions, tomato plants should be six weeks old. You should, therefore, first decide when you will be planting your tomatoes and adjust the sowing time accordingly. The planting time depends really on how cold your greenhouse becomes.

You cannot plant tomatoes outside until all danger of frost has passed, which may not be until the beginning of June in some areas, but this date can be advanced by several weeks, depending on just how much artificial protection and heat you supply. Some guidelines are summarized below. The cropping date shown in the final column will vary according to the variety.

Growing place	Approximate minimum temperature	Earliest sowing date	Earliest planting date	Earliest cropping date
Outside	At least 0°C (32°F)	15 April	1 June	1 September
Unheated greenhouse	About 5°C (41°F)	1 April	15 May	15 August
'Cold' greenhouse	7°C (45°F)	15 March	1 May	1 August
Warm greenhouse	12°C (54°F)	15 February	1 April	1 July

When you are selecting an appropriate greenhouse temperature, always remember that for every 2.8°C (5°F) rise in temperature, your heating costs will approximately double.

tip

Removing side-shoots

When you are removing the side-shoots from upright or cordon tomato plants, always take out the shoot with finger and thumb. If you use a knife, you are more likely to damage the main stem.

I grow tomatoes in the soil of my greenhouse but never seem to obtain good crops. Would I do better if I used pots?

ABOVE: Ring culture offers an excellent, disease-free way of growing tomatoes in a greenhouse.

Yes, you would almost certainly have much better results if you used pots. Some gardeners are successful in growing tomatoes in greenhouse soil beds, but they face one major risk. Diseases can easily build up in the soil, especially a debilitating problem called wilt. There is no simple control for this, and it will result in plants yielding far smaller crops than they should. It is also difficult to obtain the right balance of feeding when tomatoes are grown in this way.

You could raise your plants in normal plant pots, but much the best system is ring culture. Here, the tomatoes are grown in soil-based compost in bottomless pots or rings. These stand on a gravel bed, which is constructed by digging a trench about 40cm (16in) wide and deep, lining it with a plastic sheet and filling it with gravel. This should be kept regularly topped up with water so that it acts as a reservoir. Liquid fertilizer is applied with a watering can to the compost in the ring. Because diseases will not persist in the gravel and because the compost in the rings is renewed each year, there is no opportunity for problems to build up.

ABOVE: Blue-grey mould on stored onions is an indication of problems back at the start of the growing season.

Every time I grow onions, they turn mouldy. Where am I going wrong?

Like all other crops, onions can become mouldy for a variety of reasons, but there are two specific problems to which onions are susceptible, and these account for 90 per cent of all cases. The first, and much more serious problem, is white rot. This appears mainly on salad onions as a white mould at the base of the growing plant. If you look closely, you may see tiny white dots among the mould. Rather like clubroot on brassicas, once white mould is in your soil it is virtually impossible to eliminate it. If you want to be sure of disease-free crops, the only course of action is to set aside a bed especially for onions, using planks or railway sleepers to contain a fresh load of soil from outside your own garden. If you are prepared to tolerate some disease (and probably increasing losses), choose red-skinned onion varieties, which are rather less susceptible to white mould.

The second major disease is neck rot, which affects bulb onions after they have been harvested and are in store. A greenish mould appears around the neck of the onion. This does not persist in the soil and is easily avoided by dusting the seed or sets before planting with a systemic fungicide, preferably one containing carbendazim.

tip

Carrot root fly

This is one of the worst pests of carrots, and it also affects parsnips and parsley. The damage is caused by the larvae, which eat into the surface of the vegetables, but the best deterrent is to grow one of the newer carrot root fly-resistant varieties. The best I have grown is the all-season 'Fly Away'.

Why are my carrots always fanged and deformed despite being grown in well-riddled soil and manured with well-rotted compost?

Fanging, the term used to describe the condition that causes roots to become divided into two or more parts, is a common problem with carrots. The usual causes are a very rich soil containing fresh manure or a soil containing large clods or stones. Neither of these seem likely here, however, and the most likely reason for the trouble is a pan in the soil. A pan is a hard layer that develops 15–20cm (6–8in) down in the soil as a result of mineral matter being deposited after being washed downwards by rain. Pans are common on light soils in areas of high rainfall or in wet seasons. The solution is to make sure that the soil is double-dug every few seasons to break up the layer.

ABOVE: Perfectly shaped carrots will only be produced on soils free from clods, fresh manure or hard impervious layers.

ABOVE: Runner beans are the ideal small garden crop as they take up vertical, not horizontal space.

Which vegetables would you suggest for a small garden?

Your guiding principles in selecting vegetables for a small garden should be to choose:

* Crops you enjoy
* Crops that are particularly good when they are eaten very fresh
* Crops that are expensive to buy
* Crops that don't take up a large amount of room in return for little yield – globe artichokes and asparagus are good examples of crops that give a very poor return for the space they require

I cannot predict what your response to the first choice will be, but based on the other three, my suggestions for a small garden would be:

* Carrot – 'Fly Away'
* French bean – 'Masai'
* Lettuce – 'Little Gem', 'Tom Thumb'
* Radish – 'French Breakfast'
* Runner bean – 'Polestar' (it's often suggested, especially in seed catalogues, that non-climbing varieties of runner bean are better for small gardens, which is totally wrong; you should be making use of the vertical dimension)
* Tomato – 'Gardener's Delight', 'Sungold' and 'Incas'
* Salad leaves – including lamb's lettuce (corn salad), land cress, rocket
* Herbs – almost all

RIGHT: A number of very dark coloured potato varieties are available and many have excellent flavour.

What are the real merits of home-grown over bought vegetables?

As far as I am concerned, there are three big advantages of growing my own vegetables, all equally important. First, I can choose the varieties I want to grow. This is important because many of the vegetables you can buy in shops are chosen for reasons that have more to do with marketing than taste. Commercial varieties must be uniform, high-yielding, tough and thick-skinned; flavour usually comes well down the list.

Second, I can grow varieties in the way I choose, which is either completely organically or at least by methods that allow me to know exactly what has and has not been done to them during their production.

Third, I can eat them fresh. Almost invariably, fresh produce tastes better for the very real reason that chemical changes occur as soon as a crop is picked.

I saw some black potatoes recently. Can you tell me what variety they were?

There are several old potato varieties with very dark purple or purple-blue skins that appear superficially black. Some have a bluish coloration that extends into the flesh, while the flesh of others remains completely white. The variety you saw is probably a variety called 'Edzell Blue', which has been reintroduced for gardeners in recent years. I have grown it and found it excellent: it is very high-yielding and has a wonderful texture for mashing. You should be able to obtain it from specialist suppliers.

How long should be left between potato crops to avoid blight?

This is a question that is often asked, and the questioner usually expects that the answer will be 'years'. In fact, it is not necessary to leave as long as you might think between potato crops. The spores of the fungus that causes potato blight can survive in the soil for only a matter of days, making it a very different proposition from clubroot (see page 64) and onion white rot (see page 68). Each year new infections arise not from the soil but from spores produced on sprouts emerging from already diseased tubers. What is important, therefore, is to make sure that as many tubers as possible are dug up when the crop is harvested, that diseased tubers are not simply dumped in the garden and that any potato shoots emerging in the following year from tubers that were missed and left in the ground are dug up and destroyed promptly.

ABOVE: Although potato blight can cause serious damage, it doesn't persist in the soil.

ABOVE: Trenched celery varieties always have better flavour than self-blanching types.

Can you give some advice on growing celery and suggest a choice of varieties?

Celery isn't one of the easier garden crops, mainly because it is, by nature, a bog plant and needs plenty of water. It is, therefore, a difficult crop for soils that are very free-draining.

There are two types of celery: trenched and self-blanching. To grow trenched celery, which I believe is the better choice, you need to prepare a trench in the autumn before planting. It should be at least 40cm (16in) wide and 30cm (12in) deep, and you should add a layer of well-rotted compost or manure in the bottom. In spring sow seed into 9cm (3½in) pots in the greenhouse. Once all threat of frost has passed, plant out the young celery, taking care to disturb the roots as little as possible, in the bottom of the trench, which is slowly filled with soil. When the plants are about 30cm (12in) tall, continue to draw soil around the plants to create a ridge, so that only the tops of the plants show. You may want to wrap newspaper around the stalks to keep them clean of soil or use special celery collars, although these can attract slugs. My recommended varieties are 'Giant White' (trenched) and 'Golden Self Blanching 3' (self-blanching).

My Brussels sprouts have been spoiled by very small creatures that are right inside the buttons. What is it and how can I overcome this problem?

The creatures you have seen are grey cabbage aphids. They attack all members of the cabbage family, but they are especially troublesome on Brussels sprouts because they penetrate deep inside the buttons. The leaves become discoloured and distorted, and severe infestations will check the growth and may even kill young and weak plants. Infestations build up from July onwards and usually reach a peak in September and October. The aphids remain on the plants throughout winter and can be additionally troublesome as they spread some virus diseases to the plants.

Sadly, there is little that can be done. I would not advise you to spray the plants, and in any event, the spray would not penetrate into the buttons. Pulling up old brassicas and destroying them as soon as cropping is over will remove a good many of the eggs that would otherwise be the source of new attacks next year. Try to do this by mid-April. The plants will, of course, still be liable to attack by aphids flying in from elsewhere, and it is often on allotments, where brassicas are at different stages of growth most of the time, that the greatest problems arise.

Should I clear away all of the old vegetables in autumn?

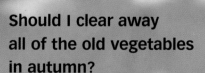

Several types of vegetables will keep well in the ground throughout winter. You should, of course, clear away any that have finished cropping, as well as the remains of any non-hardy crops, even if the frost has not finally laid them low. As much as anything, this is to remove potential hiding places in which pests, such as cabbage aphids (see above), can overwinter. All old pea and bean crops should be cleared away, as should potatoes, sweet corn, tomatoes, peppers, cucumbers, marrows, celery, celeriac, all salad crops (apart from those hardy varieties that you have planted especially for cropping in winter) and old onions (new crops of some varieties may be sown in autumn to crop next year). This leaves brassicas (cabbages, Brussels sprouts, cauliflowers and broccoli), leeks, carrots, parsnips, beetroot, swedes and turnips. These should continue to crop or at least to remain fresh, provided you have selected varieties that are described as suitable for overwintering. I find it much better to leave carrots and other root crops in the ground rather than digging them up to store.

ABOVE: Leeks are among the hardiest of vegetables and will remain reliable and fresh through the hardest winter weather.

ABOVE: Outdoor cucumbers crop well and reliably, without the pollination problems of indoor varieties.

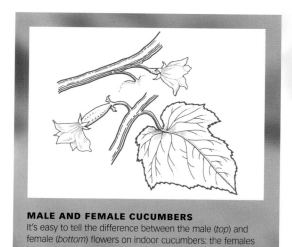

MALE AND FEMALE CUCUMBERS
It's easy to tell the difference between the male (*top*) and female (*bottom*) flowers on indoor cucumbers: the females have an elongated swelling behind the flower.

My cucumbers have cropped fairly well, but the fruit are bitter and inedible. What has gone wrong?

I assume that you have grown greenhouse cucumbers. The problem is that you have allowed the female flowers to be pollinated, and this has resulted in the unpleasant bitter taste. There are two solutions. One option is to remove the male flowers to prevent this from happening. They are easy to recognize because there is no small swelling behind the flower; on female flowers these areas will swell to produce the fruit. The second option is to choose one of the relatively modern all-female varieties. These produce few if any male flowers. Outdoor cucumber varieties do not experience the same problem and no precautions are needed.

Herbs

How long should herbs last in the garden and is it better to propagate them or buy new plants each season?

Some herbs, such as *Anethum graveolens* (dill) and *Coriandrum sativum* (coriander), are annuals and must be raised anew from seed each year. A few herbs – notably *Laurus nobilis* (bay) and *Rosmarinus officinalis* (rosemary) – are long-lasting shrubs. The rest, including *Salvia officinalis* (sage), *Thymus* spp. (thyme) and *Origanum* spp. (marjoram, oregano), are more or less woody herbaceous perennials, which will become untidy and leggy after about three years and should then be renewed.

I would recommend that you both propagate and buy new plants. You can, of course, easily renew the herbaceous types by cutting or division, but plants are relatively inexpensive to buy and there are so many different types and new forms of old favourites that it is good to ring the changes and obtain a few different ones each year.

The most important annuals and biennials, which you should certainly raise from seed each year, are the annuals dill, coriander and *Ocimum basilicum* (basil), of which many forms are now available, and the biennial *Petroselinum crispum* (parsley).

ABOVE: The ornamental sages, like this *Salvia officinalis* Purpurascens, have just as good a flavour as the plain-leaved types.

Do you agree that herbs seem to be either well flavoured or ornamental but never both?

This is a fair generalization, and *Thymus* spp. (thyme) is perhaps the best example of it. The prettiest cultivars, such as *T. citriodorus* 'Bertram Anderson' and the creeping *T.* 'Doone Valley', are quite useless in the kitchen, although I must admit that the form that I think has the best flavour, *T. vulgaris* 'Silver Posie', is also rather attractive.

Salvia spp. (sage), on the other hand, illustrates another facet of the question. There seems to me to be so little difference in the culinary qualities of the various forms that there is no reason for not choosing a really attractive one, such as the variegated *S. officinalis* 'Tricolor', rather than the rather ordinary, plain-leaved form. Similarly, the normal *Melissa officinalis* (lemon balm) is a fairly unattractive plant, whereas the golden-blotched form *M. officinalis* 'Aurea' is stunningly lovely and just as well flavoured. When it comes to *Petroselinum crispum* (parsley), however, the dark coloured and tightly curled types, such as *P. crispum* 'Moss Curled', are certainly pretty and are best for garnishing, but although they have good flavour they come a poor second to the much plainer-looking, broad-leaved *P. crispum* var. *neapolitanum* (French or Italian parsley).

Which are your top ten essential kitchen herbs?

The following herbs are those that I certainly would not want to garden and could not cook without, and they should be the core of any herb collection. Of course, your personal preferences when it comes to flavour will probably lead you to subtract a few and add others.

ABOVE: I find the range of basil varieties, like the red-leaved form seen here in a mixed planting, quite irresistible.

HERB	RECOMMENDED VARIETIES
Basil, sweet basil (*Ocimum basilicum*)	*Ocimum basilicum* 'Cinnamon' (cinnamon basil), *O. b.* 'Horapha' (Thai basil, anise basil), *O. b.* 'Napolitano', *O. b.* var. *purpurascens* (red basil, purple basil); *O. b.* var. *citriodorum* (lemon basil)
Bay laurel, sweet bay (*Laurus nobilis*)	Species
Chives (*Allium schoenoprasum*)	Species
Dill (*Anethum graveolens*)	Species
Marjoram, oregano (*Origanum* spp.)	*Origanum majorana* (sweet marjoram); *O. vulgare* (oregano, common marjoram)
Mint (*Mentha* spp.)	*Mentha gracilis* (ginger mint, red mint); *M. piperita* (peppermint); *M. spicata* (spearmint); *M. suaveolens* (apple mint), *M. s.* 'Variegata' (pineapple mint); *M. villosa* f.*alopecurioides* (Bowles' mint)
Parsley (*Petroselinum crispum*)	*Petroselinum crispum* 'Moss Curled' (curled parsley), *P. c.* var. *neapolitanum* (French parsley, Italian parsley)
Rosemary (*Rosmarinus officinalis*)	Species
Sage, common sage (*Salvia officinalis*)	*Salvia officinalis* 'Tricolor'
Thyme, garden thyme (*Thymus vulgaris*)	*Thymus herba-barona* (caraway thyme); *T. vulgaris* 'Silver Posie'

Herbs for shade
Few culinary herbs do well in shade, but there are some species that will do well in dappled or light shade and that are attractive enough for a mixed border if your herb garden is already crowded:

* *Allium schoenoprasum* (chives)
* *Angelica archangelica* (angelica)
* *Anthriscus cerefolium* (chervil)
* *Gallium odoratum* (syn. *Asperula odorata*; woodruff)
* *Levisticum officinale* (lovage)
* *Melissa officinalis* (lemon balm)
* *Myrrhis odorata* (sweet cicely)
* *Tanacetum parthenium* (syn. *Chrysanthemum parthenium*; feverfew)
* *Tanacetum vulgare* (syn. *Chrysanthemum vulgare*; tansy)
* *Tussilago farfara* (coltsfoot)

My garden gets very little sun. Are there any herbs that will thrive in shade?

Many herbs will grow in light shade, although they will be rather feeble and their flavour will not be as intense as that of herbs grown in full sun. Among the more widely grown herbs, the best ones for shade are probably *Mentha* spp. (mint) and *Salvia* spp. (sage), both of which grow naturally at the edges of woods. The true sun-lovers, such as *Thymus* spp. (thyme), will simply not grow in shade. Remember, however, that most herbs can also be grown in pots, and even a sunny windowsill will provide adequate light.

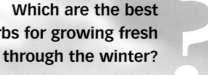

Which are the best herbs for growing fresh through the winter?

All herbs, apart from the half-hardy annuals such as *Anethum graveolens* (dill), *Coriandrum sativum* (coriander) and *Ocimum basilicum* (basil), will survive through the winter outdoors in almost all parts of Britain. Even parsley will survive in most areas, although to be sure of having fresh leaves it is worth placing a cloche over one or two plants or sowing some in a container in autumn to bring into the greenhouse or indoors. In addition, although they are strictly salad leaves rather than herbs, I do strongly recommend growing *Barbarea verna* (American land cress), which is a hardy biennial and will add a tang to your winter salads.

Herbs for containers

Most herbs are ideally suited to being grown in containers, and having a pot or two close to the back door or standing on a sheltered patio is the perfect way of having a year-round supply of really fresh leaves, even of fairly tender plants. Choose from among:

- *Allium schoenoprasum* (chives)
- *Aloysia triphylla* (syn. *A. citriodora, Lippia citriodora;* lemon verbena)
- *Anthriscus cerefolium* (chervil)
- *Hyssopus officinalis* (hyssop)
- *Laurus nobilis* (bay)
- *Myrtus communis* (myrtle)
- *Origanum vulgare* (oregano)
- *Pelargonium* 'Graveolens' (sweet- scented geranium)
- *Petroselinum crispum* (parsley)
- *Rosmarinus officinalis* (rosemary)

ABOVE RIGHT: Sink a plastic pot to its rim to prevent mint from spreading.

I have been told that it is possible to prevent mint from spreading. What should I do?

The only way to keep *Mentha* spp. (mint) under control successfully is to confine the roots, but you need a method that is not too permanent and that will allow you to remove the plants for periodic division and renewal. I usually grow the plants in 20cm (8in) diameter plastic pots. In general, I don't like using plastic pots, but in this instance they are more durable than terracotta ones and they are, in any event, largely hidden away, out of sight.

Fill the pots with potting compost – John Innes No. 2 or No. 3 is ideal – and put one mint plant in each. Sink the pots almost to their rims in the herb garden. Every autumn lift the pots from the ground and trim off any runners or roots that are threatening to escape. Replace the pot. Every third year knock each plant from its pot, renew the compost and replant a few runners to start the process again.

My thyme plants seem to have no flavour. Am I using the wrong fertilizer?

You may be using the wrong fertilizer, but it is unlikely that this is the reason your *Thymus* spp. (thyme) has no flavour. It is possible that the plants are growing in very heavy soil or in a shady site, but it is much more likely that you are growing the wrong type (see page 74). There are numerous cultivars of thyme, and most are pretty to look at but useless in the kitchen. Consider digging up your existing plants and replacing them with *Thymus vulgaris* 'Silver Posie'.

ABOVE: *Thymus* 'Doone Valley' is very pretty but won't add much to your cuisine.

What is the best way to grow herbs in the garden?

The way you grow herbs will depend largely on the type of garden you have, how interested you are in herbs for their own sake (and not simply as culinary aids) and how much space is available. At its simplest your herb garden can be a collection of containers. A rather more ambitious scheme, which would allow you to grow what I would consider the basic range of herbs for the kitchen in a straightforward way, will need an area of about 2 x 2m (6 x 6ft) as close as possible to the kitchen. Remember to plant the taller types – *Foeniculum vulgare* (fennel) and *Levisticum officinale* (lovage), for example – at the back and also, most importantly, to put in some stepping stones to provide access.

If you want a more traditional herb garden, measure accurately the area that you have available for planting and transfer the outline to scale on squared paper. Allow an area about 60 x 60cm (2 x 2ft) for each type of herb and experiment with ways in which the whole area can be attractively divided. Use small paths between the beds, and if you have room use edging plants, such as *Buxus* spp. (box), around them.

A small type of herb bed that has become popular in recent years is the cartwheel bed. Use a real cartwheel or divide a circle into equal segments with bricks or tiles and plant the individual herbs between the spokes.

LEFT: A formal herb garden is both attractive and easy to use.

My dill plants seem to disappear as soon as they are put in the garden. What am I doing wrong?

Dill is an excellent herb, but the reference in the question to putting the plants in the garden may offer a clue to their failure to thrive. *Anethum graveolens* (dill) does better when it is sown where it is to grow because it resents root disturbance. In addition, it is not reliably hardy in all areas, and it may do better if you sow the seed in the growing positions in spring, cover them with cloches until the plants are established and then thin the plants to leave 30cm (12in) between each. I usually sow a few more seeds in mid-spring to provide plants for seeding in late summer and then a few more successionally into the summer to give a regular supply of fresh young foliage.

Pick the leaves and flowerheads to use fresh. Collect the seedheads before the seeds are fully ripe and allow them to dry naturally. Take care that the plants do not become too dry between waterings or suffer other checks to their growth.

ABOVE: Dill may be used in cooking either as foliage or as seeds.

How can I keep herbs for winter use?

Herbs are best used when they are fresh, so extending the season by bringing some indoors in pots or putting cloches over them is always worthwhile. Even so, if you are to enjoy a year-round supply of your own herbs some will have to be preserved. Keep only the best quality young leaves, picking them in the early morning before the heat of the day causes the volatile oils to evaporate, and preserve them as soon after picking as possible. Freezing works well: simply place freshly picked herbs in small freezer bags or chop them up and drop them into ice cube trays of water. The latter method is useful for herbs that will later be added to soups and stews. Herbs with soft leaves, such as basil, mint and parsley, can be frozen successfully.

Drying herbs by air-drying them as you would dry flowers for arrangement does reduce the flavour, but if you have a microwave oven try spreading the herbs out on kitchen paper and 'cooking' them for no more than two or three minutes. Once dried, the leaves can be rubbed off the stalks and kept in screw-topped jars. Whichever method you choose, remember to label the herbs as you work.

An alternative method of preservation is to insert sprigs of herbs into bottles of wine vinegar or good quality oil, which will absorb the flavours. This is particularly appropriate with herbs such as rosemary and thyme.

RIGHT: The golden oregano, *Origanum vulgare* 'Aureum', is also confusingly sometimes called golden marjoram.

Can you suggest some edible flowers?

The following flowers will add colour as well as flavour to your meals: *Allium schoenoprasum* (chives), *Borago officinalis* (borage), *Calendula officinalis* (pot marigold), *Cichorium intybus* (chicory), *Cucurbita pepo* (marrow and courgette), *Origanum* spp. (marjoram), *Salvia* spp. (sage), *Scorzonera hispanica* and *Thymus* spp. (thyme). All of these plants are normal residents of the kitchen or herb garden, but there are some others that you can grow in ornamental beds and borders. Among those that are worth adding to dishes for their decorative and edible value are *Bellis perennis* (daisy), *Echium vulgare* (viper's bugloss), *Geranium pratense* (meadow cranesbill), *Rosa* cvs. (roses), *Trifolium repens* (white clover), *Tropaeolum* spp. (nasturtium) and *Viola odorata* (sweet violets).

Never, never experiment with parts of other plants unless you are sure of their safety and always avoid eating the flowers of most bulbous plants and the following:

Aconitum spp. (monkshood), *Anemone* spp. (windflower), *Aquilegia* spp. (columbine), *Clematis* spp., *Daphne* spp., *Dianthus* cvs. (pinks and carnations), *Digitalis* spp. (foxglove), *Euphorbia* spp. (spurge), *Helleborus* spp. (hellebore), *Laburnum* spp., *Papaver* spp. (poppy, even though the ripe seeds are edible) and *Taxus* spp. (yew).

Among the native flowers that look attractive but that should be avoided are *Atropa belladonna* (deadly nightshade), *Bryonia* spp. (bryony), *Hyoscyamus niger* (henbane), *Prunella* spp. (self-heal), *Ranunculus acris* (buttercup) and *Ranunculus ficaria* (celandine) and many of the umbellifers (cow parsley family). Remember, too, that the tomato-like fruits of the potato are also extremely poisonous.

ABOVE: I am always dismayed that people cut off chives flowers and inexplicably use only the stalks in their salads.

What exactly is the difference between marjoram and oregano?

Origanum is a genus of mainly Mediterranean herbs. Many of them are called marjoram, but only one, the sole British native, tends to be known as oregano. Superficially, they are all similar but differ to some degree in leaf colour, habit and fragrance. *Origanum vulgare* is known as oregano (also, confusingly, as wild marjoram); it has dark green leaves and pink or white flowers. *Origanum majorana* (sweet marjoram) is evergreen and has grey-green leaves and pink or white flowers. *Origanum onites* (pot marjoram) is semi-evergreen and has grey leaves and pink or purple flowers.

Fruit

What is the minimum area needed to provide a fairly long period of fruit for an average family?

BELOW: Fruit, like these red currants, grown as cordons takes up very little space.

You will need surprisingly little space as long as you stick to the most popular fruits.

The family's supply of apples can be met by growing a single example of what is known as a family apple tree, which is a moderately dwarfing rootstock, such as M26, grafted with two dessert cultivars (one early and one late) and one dual-purpose cultivar, such as 'Idared', which is suitable for cooking if picked early but matures into a dessert apple. For pears, plant the cultivar 'Conference' two-dimensionally as an espalier, and for plums grow 'Victoria, also two-dimensionally but fan-trained against a wall or fence. Finally, have two plants each of red currants and white currants and gooseberries as double cordons and a single plant of the compact blackcurrant *Ribes nigrum* 'Ben Sarek'. All these should take up no more than about 9 square metres (less than 100 square feet).

What is a cordon?

A cordon is a plant that is grown in such a way that one, two or sometimes three shoots are trained upwards, while the remainder of the shoots are cut off and the side-shoots are cut back annually to just above two buds from their base. It is an excellent way of growing a number of different types of fruit or different forms of the same fruit within a limited area, and among the plants especially amenable to cordon training are apples, red currants and white currants (but not blackcurrants) and gooseberries.

tip

Choosing a rootstock

The rootstocks on to which apple trees are grafted will determine the ultimate size of the tree as well as the shape into which you can train it. There are several, ranging from the dwarfing M27 to the vigorous M25, but the most often used are:

- ❋ M27 – suitable for bushes, cordons, spindlebushes, step-overs and tubs
- ❋ M9 – suitable for bushes, cordons, fans, pyramids, spindlebushes and step-overs
- ❋ M26 and MM106 – suitable for bushes, cordons, espaliers, fans, pyramids and spindlebushes
- ❋ MM111 – suitable for espaliers, fans, half-standards and standards

Which cultivars of garden fruit would you recommend?

There are many cultivars of almost every kind of garden fruit, and there are hundreds of apples. Each has merits and disadvantages, but in drawing up the list that follows I have attempted to cover a range of early, mid-season and late types where appropriate. I have also included those that store or, in the case of soft fruit, freeze well and, most importantly, those that have a good flavour, which is enhanced when they are picked fresh.

* Apple (cooking) – 'Bramley's Seedling' (triploid – i.e., requires two other pollinators), 'Howgate Wonder'
* Apple (dessert, in order of maturing) – 'Beauty of Bath', 'Discovery', 'Redsleeves', 'Fortune', 'James Grieve' (dual purpose), 'Greensleeves', 'Ellison's Orange', 'Sunset', 'Blenheim Orange' (dual purpose), 'Jupiter' (triploid), 'Spartan', 'Worcester Pearmain', 'Crispin' (triploid), 'Idared', 'Tydeman's Late Orange', 'Kent', 'Golden Delicious'
* Apricot – 'Moorpark'
* Blackberry – 'Loch Ness' (early to mid-season), 'Ashton Cross' (mid-season)
* Blackcurrant – 'Wellington XXX' (early to mid-season), 'Ben Sarek' (mid-season), 'Ben Lomond' (mid-season to late)
* Cherry (bitter) – 'Morello'
* Cherry (sweet) – 'Stella'
* Damson – 'Merryweather'
* Fig – 'Brown Turkey'
* Gage – 'Oullin's Golden Gage' (early)
* Gooseberry – 'Careless' (early to mid-season), 'Invicta' (early to mid-season), 'Lord Derby' (late)
* Grape vine – 'Schiava Grossa' (syn. 'Black Hamburgh'), 'Siegerrebe'
* Hybrid berries – Tayberry
* Nectarine – 'Lord Napier'
* Peach – 'Peregrine', 'Rochester'
* Pear – 'Conference', 'Beurré Hardy', 'Williams Bon Chrétien', 'Doyenné du Comice'
* Plum – 'Victoria' (mid-season), 'Marjorie's Seedling' (late)
* Raspberry – 'Glen Moy' (early), 'Glen Prosen' (mid-season), 'Malling Admiral' (late), 'Autumn Bliss' (autumn)
* Red currant – 'Red Lake'
* Strawberry – 'Aromel' (autumn), 'Cambridge Favourite' (mid-season), 'Pegasus' (late)
* White currant – 'Versailles Blanche'

ABOVE TOP: Training apples as cordons, like 'Kidd's Orange Red' and 'Katja', shown here, enables you to grow many varieties in a very small area.

ABOVE: 'Victoria' is without equal as an all-round, easy to grow plum.

Will my very vigorous old standing apple trees benefit from pruning?

No, they will not. Pruning such trees will simply induce them to produce even more shoot growth. You need to restrict their vigour by allowing grass to grow around the base of the trunk and by giving no fertilizer other than an annual dressing of sulphate of potash, which will encourage blossom at the expense of more leafy growth.

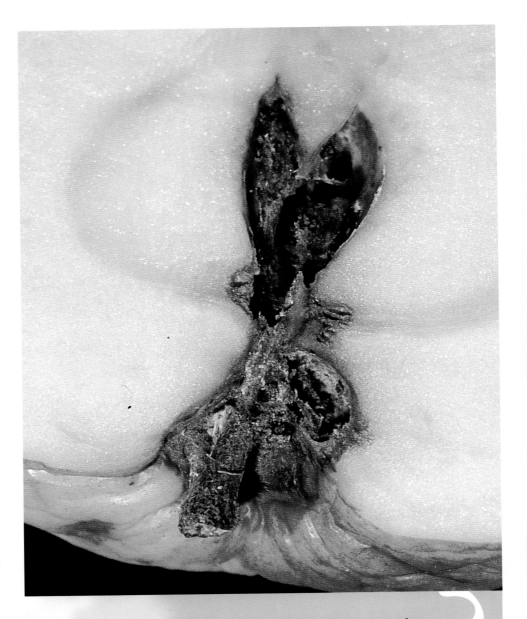

RIGHT: Codling moth damage is largely invisible until the fruit is cut open.

Why do my apples have maggots inside them every year?

This is nothing serious. The maggots are the caterpillars of the codling moth, and they burrow into the young fruit very close to the 'eye', where they cannot easily be seen. They occasionally also attack pears, and a similar pest, the plum fruit moth, affects plums. After feeding for some time, the larvae eat their way out of the fruit and pupate in cracks in the bark of the tree. Adults hatch out in the following year. You will never control them all, but the numbers can be reduced by hanging proprietary pheromone traps in the fruit trees. These traps, which are obtainable at garden centres, contain a chemical that mimics the insect's sex hormone and lures male moths on to a sticky platform from which there is no escape.

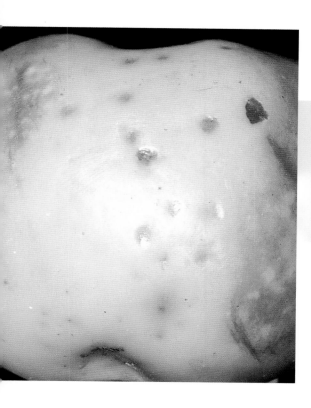

LEFT: The spots caused by bitter pit look superficially like a disease, but in reality are caused by calcium deficiency.

All the apples in my garden have black spots within the flesh. What is wrong with them?

The problem is called bitter pit, and it is caused by a shortage of the element calcium in the fruit. As you might imagine, this is especially common on acidic soils, which do not naturally contain lime, and it is exacerbated in very dry weather because a shortage of water means that any calcium that is available is not transported around the tree. If your soil is naturally acidic, it would be worth applying lime around the trees, especially if you have an apple such as 'Bramley's Seedling', which is particularly susceptible to the problem.

How should I prune my newly bought apple tree?

BELOW: The early stages of pruning a young apple tree are critical for the way in which it develops in future years.

Apple trees are normally bought as 'maidens' or 'maiden whips' – that is, as one-year-old trees consisting of the growth that was made during the first season after the fruiting cultivar was grafted on to the rootstock (see page 80). Some maidens are 'feathered' – that is, they have lateral shoots along their stems. In all cases, however, the early pruning is important because it will dictate the overall form of your tree in years to come.

After planting a maiden tree in winter, cut back the leading shoot by up to one-third or to the required height, cutting above a plump bud. At the same time, completely remove any side-shoots. In the second winter, choose from three to five strong side-shoots that are growing at a wide, spreading angle to form permanent branches, and cut these back by between one-half (the more vigorous ones) and two-thirds (the less vigorous ones) to just above an outward-pointing bud. Completely remove all other side-shoots.

By the third winter the branches will have grown strong new shoots. Choose from six to ten of these to retain as a permanent framework, and cut them back by one-half to two-thirds, cutting just above outward-pointing buds. At the same time, cut back any side-shoots growing inside the framework to just above four buds from the base to encourage the development of spurs. Leave some laterals on the outside of the bush unpruned to form flower buds for 'renewal pruning' and remove any unwanted branches completely. This process can be repeated in the fourth winter, by which time the framework of the tree should be complete and no further pruning of leaders should be necessary.

Will adding rotten apples to the heap spread disease through my compost?

No, it will not. The commonest of the fungi that cause apple rot will not affect other plants, and the spores will, in any event, be killed if your compost heap is functioning properly and maintaining a high temperature. Try not to allow rotten apples to hang on the trees over winter, however, because they certainly can harbour the fungus and increase the amount of disease in the following year.

tip

Picking apples

Never pick an apple too soon; it needs as much sun as possible to develop its flavour and build up its reserves and skin so that it will keep well. Never tug an apple from the tree; a ripe apple will come away if you support it in the palm of your hand and turn it gently. Never pick an apple without a stalk; this will simply leave a hole through which decay can take hold.

I have been told that my apple trees need a pollinator to crop properly. What does this mean?

Many tree fruit cultivars are not self-fertile, which means that one tree is not sufficient to pollinate the blossom, without which there can be no fruit. In many instances, although each individual flower has both male and female parts, achieving a satisfactory pollination requires pollen from another flower. With most fruit that is all there is to it. Peaches, apricots, some cherries, some plums and all soft fruit will produce fruit perfectly well on their own. They are said to be self-fertile, and you require only one tree or one bush of each type of fruit. With some plants, although not with many fruit, you will fare better with two trees, although they should still be of the same cultivar.

With a great many fruit trees, including very many apples, however, you require not only two trees but two trees of a different cultivar in order for the best or even for any pollination to occur. And this is where trouble starts, because the trees must be of two compatible types. Apple cultivars are arranged into pollination groups, and cultivars within one group will pollinate others in the same group and also those in adjacent groups, but not the remainder. By and large, the groupings reflect flowering time, so if two apple trees flower at more or less the same time, it is likely that they will pollinate each other. Choose cultivars within the same pollination group if possible, therefore or, failing that, from adjoining groups (your nursery will advise you).

Finally, before leaving apples, it is necessary to point out that a very few cultivars, such as 'Crispin' and 'Bramley's Seedling', require not one, but two additional cultivars. They are said to be triploid. Among apples, a few cultivars, such as 'James Grieve', will pollinate pretty well everything else.

LEFT: A single apple tree will produce a crop only if there is a suitable pollinator tree nearby.

What is the secret of growing good pears?

In short, good soil and sunshine. Although they are close relatives of apples, pears are much less hardy, and they are seldom successful in the far north or in cold, exposed sites. Pears are big plants, with a reputation for being slow to come into cropping – the old saying about planting 'pears for your heirs' has some foundation in fact.

For the best and most reliable crop, I would grow pears as espaliers, a training form to which they are especially suited and that looks very attractive. This will occupy less ground area than a free-standing tree, the wall or other support against which the pear is grown will give some protection, and the crop will be easier to pick. Choose from 'Conference', 'Beurré Hardy', 'Williams Bon Chrétien' and 'Doyenné du Comice' and obtain plants grafted on to a rootstock called 'Quince C', which will limit their vigour and result in a crop at a younger age.

LEFT: The espalier is a training system that offers pears the additional warmth they need to succeed.

Every year my peach tree has diseased leaves and no fruit. What can I do?

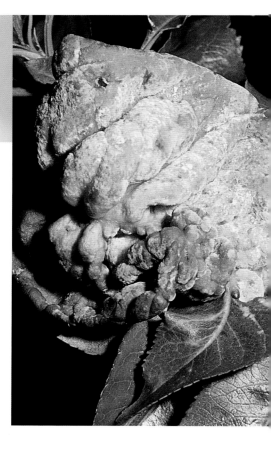

The probable solution to your problem would be to switch to growing another type of fruit. Diseased leaves on peaches almost invariably mean that the plant is infected with peach leaf curl. The foliage gradually puckers, becomes covered with a powdery white growth, then slowly turns first red, then brown and shrivelled. Finally, the leaves drop.

Peaches and nectarines everywhere are extremely susceptible to this problem, although it is especially bad in damp localities and in wet seasons. Peaches growing in conservatories generally escape damage. No chemical controls are very effective, and if you enjoy this type of stone fruit, my advice is to change to apricots, which are virtually unaffected by the problem and which are also, incidentally, much hardier than many people imagine.

RIGHT: Peach leaves affected by leaf curl disease are distorted and turn white as the fungal spores develop.

tip

Rootstocks for plums, gages and damsons

As with apples, plums, gages and damsons are grown on rootstocks that control the ultimate size of the trees and the shapes into which they can be trained.

- ❀ 'Pixy' – suitable for plum and gage bushes, cordons, espaliers, fans, spindlebushes and pyramids to about 2.4m (8ft) tall
- ❀ 'St Julien A' – suitable for plum, gage and damson bushes, cordons, espaliers, fan, spindlebushes and pyramids to about 4m (13ft) tall
- ❀ 'Brompton' – suitable for half-standard and standard trees to 4.5m (15ft)
- ❀ 'Myrobalan B' – suitable for some half-standard and standard trees to 4.5m (15ft) but not universally compatible

What is the difference between plums, gages and damsons and which should I grow?

These are all similar stone fruits. There is very little difference between gages and plums, which belong to the same species, *Prunus domestica*, although most plums are relatively large, oval and generally purple, while gages tend to be smaller, rounded and yellow or green. Damsons belong to a related species, *Prunus institia*, and are smaller, purple and less sweet; they are not usually eaten fresh.

All three are easy to grow because all damsons and many of the best plums and gages are self-fertile, so only one tree is needed. They are also hardy – damsons extremely so – and they require very little pruning after the early, formative stages. The only real disadvantage is that no truly dwarfing rootstocks are obtainable, the best for garden use being 'St Julien A' and 'Pixy'. They may be grown as free-standing trees or trained as fans. See page 81 for some recommended cultivars.

I've been told that my trees need tar oil. What is this and why should I apply it to my trees?

Tar oil is a type of insecticide that is especially valuable for eradicating pests, such as aphids, which spend the winter hiding in the crevices of the bark. It is used most commonly on fruit trees and bushes, but it can be applied to any deciduous woody plants. It must not, however, be used on evergreens because it harms the foliage, and for this reason it is always applied in winter, when deciduous plants have shed their leaves.

Do not apply tar oil in very frosty weather, always wear protective goggles and take care not to allow too much spray to splash on to grass or other greenery; the damage will not be permanent but it will be disfiguring.

ABOVE: In the British climate, figs require two seasons to produce a mature crop.

I have had a fig for three years, but the fruit dropped off before they ripened. What can I do to make sure that I have figs to eat?

It is possible that the plant is short of water, but I suspect that it is more likely that you are failing to understand how fig fruits develop. Figs are native to warm, sunny areas such as Turkey, Cyprus and the Caucasus, and in areas with long summers embryo figs appear in late summer. In the following spring and summer these embryo figs grow to maturity, and at the same time a second crop of fruit appears further along the stems. This second crop never ripens and generally falls; if they do not fall, the fruits should be removed so that the plant's energies can be concentrated on ripening the previous year's fruit. Then a third crop, the embryo figs, appears on the ends of the stems, and these are the following year's fruits.

Although figs are hardy, British summers are not usually long enough for the new embryo fruits to form and for the existing embryo fruits to mature. Growing a fig in a 30cm (12in) container, which can be brought under cover in the coldest part of the year, might help, as would growing the tree against a wall or fence, which would provide some additional protection. Remember, too, that when a fig is planted in the open garden, the tree's roots should be restricted in some way if fruits are to be produced. The usual method is to plant the fig in an open-bottomed trough about 60 x 60cm (2 x 2ft).

I like strawberries but am told they take up a great deal of room. Is this true?

ABOVE: Strawberries are tempting to grow but require a good deal of work, and much more room, than you would imagine.

Yes, strawberries do take a lot of room in the garden, and although you will see advertisements for strawberry containers that give the impression that you can obtain a crop from minimal space, they are misleading. You can grow a small number of strawberries in a container for a season, but you should not expect more.

There are three main problems with strawberries: they produce relatively few fruit per plant; they cover a great deal of ground; and – a fact that is largely unappreciated – they are best treated as annuals and will not crop reliably for more than three years when grown in the same soil. This means that they must be grown on a rotation system, like vegetables, and unless you have a great deal of spare room in your kitchen garden, I would devote your energies elsewhere.

Can you give some advice on selecting and planting trouble-free raspberries?

Raspberries do not generally crop well on the light soil in my own garden, so any that do fare well there are likely to be pretty good in most other places. I will suggest two cultivars that I have found reliable: the summer-fruiting 'Glen Moy' and the autumn-fruiting 'Autumn Bliss'.

For successful planting, which is best done in late autumn, follow the guidelines below:

* Choose the warmest, sunniest spot available; raspberries will tolerate only very light shade.
* Dig a trench, ideally orientated north–south, about 45cm (18in) deep for the planting row and fork in plenty of well-rotted organic matter.
* Plant the canes or 'stools' 38–45cm (15–18in) apart, with the upper part of the roots about 5cm (2in) deep on top of the carefully firmed contents of the trench. Any new white cane buds should be just at soil level. Planting deeper than this may discourage new cane production.
* Move the canes slightly as the soil is refilled around them to make sure than no air pockets are left and firm the soil carefully with your foot. The soil should slope slightly away from the canes.
* Allow 40cm (16in) between each plant and 1.5m (5ft) between each row.
* Water the canes well, top with a mulch of compost and cut back the canes (if this was not done by the nursery) to just above a bud about 25cm (10in) above soil level.

LEFT: The outstanding autumn variety 'Autumn Bliss' has revolutionized the growing of late season raspberries.

I'm baffled by the various types of soft fruit and by words like early, mid-season and late. What are the differences?

The expression 'soft fruit' is used to describe both bush and cane fruit and strawberries. Bush fruit includes red currants, white currants, blackcurrants and gooseberries and blueberries. Cane fruit includes raspberries, blackberries and hybrid berries.

Almost all types of soft fruit, except red- and white currants, are described as 'early', 'mid-season' and 'late', and these terms describe the time of cropping. It is important to remember, however, that the cropping time is relative not absolute. In cold areas, for instance, an early variety may be beginning to crop at the same time as a mid-season variety is fully mature in a warmer district. If you do live in a cold area, concentrate on mid-season and late varieties. This is important because, although the terms relate to cropping time, they also reflect flowering time, and an early blossoming variety will always be prone to damage from spring frosts. Cropping sequences are suggested in the list of recommended varieties on page 81.

How could my gooseberry bush lose all its foliage in the course of a single night?

ABOVE: Gooseberry sawfly larvae may strip the foliage but leave the fruit unharmed.

Very easily if it had been attacked by the larvae of the gooseberry sawfly, which will reduce the leaves to skeletons in just a few hours. The female insects lay eggs in slits made alongside the main leaf veins on the undersides of leaves, and the eggs hatch about a week later. All the brownish, caterpillar-like larvae emerge simultaneously and feed voraciously. Red and white currants are also attacked, and it is very important to keep a close, almost daily check on the plants in late spring for the first signs of damage. If the larvae are seen, pinch them off by hand or use a safe insecticide. Single attacks, even if the plants are almost entirely defoliated, won't affect them in the long term, but if the attacks are repeated year after year both cropping and vigour will quickly decline.

LEFT TOP: The tayberry is much the best of the modern raspberry-blackberry hybrids.

LEFT BELOW: Loganberries are among the older hybrid fruits, and still worth growing if you choose the thornless variety.

I enjoy soft fruit. What do you think of the newer hybrid berries?

Almost all the hybrid berries are crosses between raspberries and blackberries, and all are grown and trained in the same way as blackberries. Some have been known for many years – the familiar loganberry being an accidental cross of nineteenth-century origin – but recently plant breeders have deliberately produced many more. I have grown most of them, and the following are my top five:

* Boysenberry (thornless form) – the large, purple fruits are like elongated raspberries; it is early, vigorous, drought tolerant and a good plant for light, free-draining soils.
* King's Acre Berry – the medium-sized fruit are very dark red to black; it is early, fairly vigorous and thorny.
* Loganberry LY654 (thornless form) – the large fruit are dark red; it is early and fairly vigorous.

* Tayberry – the large, dark red fruit are the best of the raspberry–blackberry hybrids; it is early, moderately vigorous and thorny, but not very hardy and less good for exposed gardens.
* Tummelberry – a hybrid between two tayberries, it has large, dark red fruit; it is early (but slightly later than the tayberry), moderately vigorous and thorny, but hardier than the tayberry so better for more exposed gardens.

How feasible would it be to grow a grape vine in my greenhouse yet still have tomato crops too?

The arrangement is not ideal, but it is possible to have both grapes and tomatoes in the same greenhouse. It is a problem that faces many gardeners, especially if they have a conservatory where there is an established grape vine but they want to grow other crops. The overall effect can be very attractive, but a little extra work is involved.

Ideally, the vine should be planted outside the greenhouse and trained in through a hole in the wall (see page 34). The tomatoes must be grown in some form of container, such as ring culture pots, and not in soil beds where they would be competing with the vine for moisture. Assuming that the vine is carefully trained and pruned, its foliage will take over the role of normal greenhouse shading, which will therefore be unnecessary. The only significant problems may come in the second half of the season when the vine begins to drip sap and honeydew on to the tomatoes and on this, in turn, black sooty mould develops. You may have to bring the tomato cropping season to a slightly premature end.

Greenhouses

What are the most important factors to consider when siting a new greenhouse?

Always bear in mind that the purpose of a greenhouse is to provide warmth so that plants will grow more quickly, in sheltered conditions and free from any danger of frost. A greenhouse must, therefore, be positioned to optimize the warming effect of the sun, and, because warmth is related to light, it must be in the position where it will be exposed to the greatest intensity of sunlight. There are other considerations, too, and you should try to incorporate as many of the following as possible:

* Choose a site away from shade.
* Orientate the greenhouse east–west; this provides more uniform illumination that the traditional north–south axis.
* Choose a spot as far as possible from deciduous trees; the leaves will block the drainage gutters and, if they are close enough, honeydew will drip from them on to the glass.
* Choose a level site.
* Prepare proper foundations, at least 20cm (8in) deep, to which the structure is firmly secured and make sure that a wooden greenhouse is not in contact with the soil.

Ventilating your greenhouse
Even in winter you will need to ventilate your greenhouse, and few greenhouses have sufficient means of ventilation. Louvred windows, provided they fit well, are useful. Automatic vent openers, which operate when the temperature inside the greenhouse reaches a specified level, are very useful and easy to fit. Domestic extractor fans can also be used, but make sure that you fit one that is suitable for the size of your greenhouse.

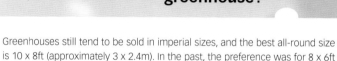

What is the optimum size for an average garden greenhouse?

Greenhouses still tend to be sold in imperial sizes, and the best all-round size is 10 x 8ft (approximately 3 x 2.4m). In the past, the preference was for 8 x 6ft (2.4 x 2m), but this is a bit small to be truly versatile.

Draw up a list of all the uses to which your greenhouse will be put – seed sowing, tomato growing, overwintering stock plants, raising plants for the house and so on – work out the area that you require and then double it. Once you have a greenhouse, you will be astonished at how addictive greenhouse gardening can become.

Do you prefer wood or aluminium greenhouses?

Wood, but partly that is because I love anything made of wood, and I have an old house and garden with which a bright, silver-coloured aluminium structure would look inappropriate. The pros and cons are fairly easily summarized:

WOOD	ALUMINIUM
Relatively expensive	Relatively inexpensive
Moderate maintenance (much less if unpainted red cedar; much more if painted wood of any type)	Low maintenance
Warms up slowly but retains heat well and cools down slowly	Warms up quickly but retains heat less well and cools down quickly
Easy to fit attachments, such as insulation	Can be tricky to fit attachments, especially anything not custom made
Flexible and unlikely to be damaged by strong winds	Rigid and may be damaged in gales
Environmentally unobtrusive	Environmentally obtrusive

If, however, you are prepared to pay (considerably) more, some greenhouse manufacturers now offer structures made of coated aluminium in period designs, and these have the appearance of a painted wooden greenhouse but minimal maintenance requirements

TOP RIGHT: Aluminium greenhouses are now the choice for most gardeners, although they aren't always appropriate for the gardens of old houses.

BOTTOM RIGHT: Wooden greenhouses may require more maintenance but have some advantages over aluminium structures.

How effective are the inexpensive small, lean-to greenhouses?

These small structures are much better than nothing, and, like all lean-to greenhouses, they benefit from the warmth of the adjoining building. Because they are so small, however, they tend to cool down quickly and so need good insulation. Nonetheless, if you have limited space or resources, they offer an excellent step up from the kitchen window sill.

What is the best type of floor for my new greenhouse?

ABOVE: There is no real substitute for gravel as a greenhouse floor.

Ask most gardening experts and they will answer this question with 'concrete', which is easy to clean and disinfect, durable and pest and weed free and which, moreover, provides a firm surface on which to stand.

I have used concrete-floored greenhouses, however, and have found them boring to look at, tiring to stand on and, frankly, unnecessary. I much prefer a layer of gravel or stone chippings, abut 2cm (5in) deep, over firmed soil. Weeds are not a problem, and a once- or twice-a-year watering with a garden disinfectant takes care of any pests and diseases. The floor is pleasing to look at and sets off plants perfectly, it is easy on the feet, and it is free draining. If you want a slightly firmer area for paths in a large greenhouse use bricks.

Should I be worried about the condensation that arises because of the insulation in my greenhouse?

Some condensation between the insulation sheet and the glass is inevitable. It will become a problem only if the insulation is not removed once a year so that you can clean the glass properly. If the glass is not cleaned, a film of green algal growth and moulds will build up and impair the light transmission and threaten the health of your plants.

What type of staging do you recommend?

In general you should use the same material for staging as for the greenhouse itself, although wooden staging should be made from hardwood rather than red cedar, which, although durable, really is not strong enough to support the considerable weight of many pots filled with compost. If you are growing alpines (see page 56), bear in mind that the weight of a gravel bench will be enormous, and unless you intend to use very stout timbers, an angular metal construction may be better.

Is it worthwhile installing a greenhouse heating system?

The answer must be yes if you want to obtain the maximum benefit from what is bound to have been a big investment in building a greenhouse in the first place. An unheated greenhouse can be used for storing dormant plants, such as dahlias and chrysanthemums, over winter but only if they (and the greenhouse) are well insulated and so will escape frost damage. You will not be able to have any tender plants in growth in winter, and the gain in time for your plants in spring will be small. Having a heated propagator in an unheated greenhouse certainly offers a significant advance, but best of all is space heating, ideally with easily controlled electric heaters. The table below summarizes the benefits provided by different levels of heating:

ABOVE: A thermostatically controlled electric fan heater is much the simplest option for most greenhouses.

MINIMUM TEMPERATURE IN GREENHOUSE	EXTRA SCOPE OFFERED AND LIMITATIONS
2°C (36°F)	Overwintered tender plants, such as pelargoniums, non-hardy fuchsias and dahlia tubers, will not be damaged by frost, although barely anything will grow if the daytime temperature rises very little above this level
7°C (45°F)	Winter lettuce can be grown, and cuttings and young plants can be maintained in good order
15°C (59°F)	A daytime temperature of around 17°C (63°F), together with supplementary lighting, will allow you to raise winter tomatoes and cucumbers
20°C (68°F)	Tropical plants can be grown all year round

On balance, a minimum temperature of 7°C (45°F) will be found most practical and economical. Remember that every 2.4°C (5°F) rise in temperature approximately doubles the heating costs.

What are the pros and cons of insulating a greenhouse with bubble plastic?

So far, I have not found many cons, and I now use bubble plastic on my greenhouse all year round for the following reasons. In summer a greenhouse becomes too hot and some method is needed to cool it down. Ventilation is important, of course, but you must also cut down the amount of sunlight entering the greenhouse. The conventional way to do this is with shading paint – that is, with special white paint (not normal emulsion) that is put on the outside of the glass in the spring, is not washed off by rain but can be wiped off with a cloth at the end of the season. When the paint is taken off at the end of summer, bubble film insulation is put in its place. This all seemed to me to be too complicated, and I decided to see if the bubble film would keep out heat in summer just as well as it keeps it in in winter. It does.

RIGHT: Double film bubble plastic insulation will keep a greenhouse cool in summer as well as warm in winter.

tip

Using a cold frame to harden off

During the first week leave the frame cover half-open in the day time but closed at night. In the second week keep the cover fully open during the day and half-open at night.

RIGHT: Cloches are not a substitute for a greenhouse, but they do give a head start to early crops, like these broad beans.

Do you think the average gardener really needs a cold frame?

Yes, gardeners need a cold frame whether or not they also have a greenhouse. It is one of the most undervalued items of gardening equipment, serving several purposes:

* It provides hardening-off space for plants that have been raised in warmth (either in the greenhouse or indoors) before they are put out in the garden.
* It provides a protected area for striking cuttings, especially hardwood cuttings, in late autumn and winter.
* It acts as storage space for plants such as chrysanthemums that are unreliable in many areas if left in the garden over winter.
* It will enable you to grow melons or similar, barely hardy crops.

Do you think it is worth installing greenhouse lighting?

Not many gardeners use greenhouse lighting, but it can be valuable if you are heating the greenhouse to grow plants over winter or if you want to obtain good seedling growth in late winter or early spring.

There are a number of important factors to consider when you are choosing a lighting system, but basically you need one that offers the maximum amount of light output within the wavelengths required for photosynthesis while having low installation and running costs. Much the most efficient are low-pressure sodium lamps, but they are among the most expensive to install, and most gardeners opt for the relatively inefficient but cheap low-pressure, mercury discharge fluorescent tubes. Whichever system you select, however, do check carefully that its output really will be cost-effective.

How useful are cloches?

I find cloches very useful indeed, mainly in extending the season for vegetable and salad crops at the beginning and end of the season. They make it possible to sow or plant out sooner and to harvest later. Although various models of plastic cloche are now available, I much prefer traditional glass and wire structures. Remember, however, that while cloches provide localized warming of the environment around the plants, they do not in any sense replicate the warming effect of a greenhouse, even a greenhouse without artificial heat. Don't be tempted to put out tender plants too soon, therefore.

I always seem to be hearing the expression 'greenhouse hygiene'. What exactly does it mean?

At the very least, it means being neat and tidy. A greenhouse that is cluttered with rubbish and the remains of old plants will harbour both pests and diseases. As leaves turn yellow on plants, pull them off and dispose of them. And be scrupulous at the end of each season in clearing away the remains of tomatoes and other annual crops. Do not allow used pots to accumulate and do not use the greenhouse as a shed for storing compost and other items. Once old plants have been thrown out, temporarily remove the remainder and scrub the whole greenhouse structure with hot water and soap, spray with a proprietary garden disinfectant and then wash clean again. This will help eliminate any pests that are hiding in cracks and crevices from where they may attack next year's plants.

ABOVE: There are few more depressing sights in gardening than a neglected greenhouse; try to use yours all year round.

RIGHT: Sticky yellow cards offer a very simple means of trapping insect pests.

I have a problem with pests in the greenhouse. Do you think that biological control would be likely to help?

Yes, you probably would find that biological controls would be very helpful. The range of these controls available for garden use is now considerable, and listed on the right are those that are suitable for the greenhouse. Remember, however, that if you use a biological control for one pest, you will not be able to use chemicals to control other types of pests because the insecticide will affect the biological control agents.

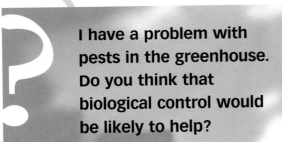

PEST	BIOLOGICAL CONTROL AGENT
Aphids	*Aphidoletes aphidimyza* – predatory midge
Aphids	*Aphidius matricariae* – parasitic wasp
Aphids and other pests	*Chrysoperla carnea* – lacewing
Caterpillars	*Bacillus thuringiensis* – bacterium
Fungus gnats	*Hypoaspis miles* – predatory mite
Glasshouse whitefly	*Encarsia formosa* – parasitic wasp
Glasshouse whitefly	*Delphastus pusillus* – predatory ladybird beetle
Mealy bug	*Cryptoleamus montrouzieri* – predatory ladybird beetle
Red spider mites	*Phytoseiulus persimilis* – predatory mite
Scale insects (soft scale only)	*Metaphycus helvolus* – parasitic wasp
Thrips	*Amblyseius cucumeris* – predatory mite
Vine weevil larvae	*Heterorhabditis* spp. – predatory nematode

Can I put anything in my water butt to stop algae from growing on my greenhouse pots?

Algal growth is not itself parasitic, but it will use up fertilizer intended for the plants and it can block the compost surface, impeding aeration. More importantly, where there is algal growth there are probably disease spores and pests. Potassium permanganate crystals (sometimes called Condy's Crystals) will have some effect in disinfecting the water in a rain butt, while a fine filter (such as a pair of old tights) over the mouth of the downpipe through which water enters the butt will help to lessen the initial contamination.

I prefer the safer principle, however, of not using water from a rain butt on plants, especially on young seedlings, inside the greenhouse where the enhanced warmth is likely to exacerbate any problems that are present.

ABOVE: Trickle irrigation, with one nozzle per plant, is the ideal greenhouse watering system.

What is the best way to keep greenhouse plants healthy when I go away on holiday?

It is pointless and unwise to try to ensure that your plants will receive the same overall attention as when you are present to tend them. Instead, concentrate on keeping them watered. If you do not have a neighbour who will water regularly for you, the ideal arrangement is a trickle irrigation system, preferably operating from the mains but alternatively from a reservoir. This will deliver water, drop by drop, to each plant, wherever it is positioned. Installing such a system requires advance planning. A second option for individual pots on the bench is to stand them all on a water-absorbent capillary mat, linked by a wick to a small reservoir.

For tomatoes, which require large amounts of water, the ideal system is ring culture, but this, too, will have needed advance planning. Tomatoes in growing bags are the most vulnerable to drying out, but small, plug-in 'tanks' of water, which deliver water slowly through a small pipe pushed into the side of the growing bag, offer a good first-aid option.

I would like to grow orchids in my greenhouse. Can I do this without having to provide heating?

Although many people think that heat and orchids are synonymous, many species of orchid grow in cool, temperate climates, including that of Britain. Paradoxically, however, these are not the species that I suggest you try because they are all terrestrial, and this group, with the main exception of pleiones, is tricky to cultivate. My advice would be to opt for the easiest of the warm-climate, epiphytic orchids, the cymbidiums, because they are tolerant of low temperatures in winter, provided, that is, they remain a few degrees above freezing. This should be possible to attain if the greenhouse is well insulated and in a sheltered spot.

Use a proprietary orchid compost in clay pots and only pot on the orchids to a larger container when the mass of bulbs really threatens to break the pot apart. Water carefully, allowing the compost almost to dry out in winter and never become waterlogged in summer. There is no need to give fertilizer until growth begins to show in spring, but from then on, apply liquid fertilizer about once every ten days.

RIGHT: Cymbidium hybrids, like these 'Pink Perfection', are among the easiest and most beautiful of orchids for the home greenhouse.

Is it a good idea to store overwintering plants like dahlias in the greenhouse?

Dahlias should be overwintered in a greenhouse only if it is relatively cool – that is, if it has a minimum temperature no higher than 7°C (45°F; see page 95) – otherwise the plants will start into growth prematurely and become weakened in the process.

If the greenhouse is cool enough, dust the tubers with sulphur to minimize rotting, surround them with dry potting compost or other organic matter and store them under the staging in boxes (see also page 130).

RIGHT: *Passiflora antioquiensis* is one of the many wonderful passion flowers suitable for a conservatory.

How can I turn my greenhouse into an alpine house?

This is a very easy process, and it is certainly the least expensive way of deriving year-round benefit from your greenhouse because you need no artificial heat. Make sure that the greenhouse is in the best possible site (see page 92). Make sure, too, that it receives the maximum amount of sunlight, because relatively few alpine plants are shade tolerant.

The only structural alterations will be to provide additional ventilation. It is almost impossible to have too much ventilation for alpines – think of the wind blowing on mountain tops – and in some ways, it is better to think of an alpine house more as a giant, open-ended cloche than as a greenhouse. One other requirement is to provide some very strong staging, which must be stronger than most normal greenhouse staging because the most satisfactory and aesthetically pleasing way of growing alpines is with their pots sunk to the rim in a gravel bed. The weight of several centimetres of gravel is considerable.

LEFT: An alpine house requires little more than very good ventilation and very strong staging.

Can you suggest some plants for my new double-glazed conservatory?

Assuming that your conservatory remains pretty warm and pretty dry all year round, the following are my top ten suggestions for flowers and foliage. I suggest that you be adventurous and grow some of the plants that would be too large or inappropriate for the house, but avoid such tempting subjects as bougainvilleas, ferns and other thin-leaved species, which will turn unattractively brown without a moist atmosphere.

- *Abutilon* spp. (flowering maple, Indian mallow)
- *Aeonium* spp.
- *Agapanthus* spp. (African blue lily)
- *Brugmansia* spp. (angels' trumpets)
- *Caladium* spp. (angel wings)
- *Citrus* spp.
- *Clianthus* spp. (glory pea)
- *Gloriosa superba*
- *Hibiscus* spp.
- Orchids
- *Passiflora* spp. (passion flower)

Water gardens

BELOW: Pools are long-term, complex garden features, so it's very important to position them correctly.

What is the best position in a garden to place a pool?

The first criterion is a site that has maximum exposure to sunshine. No pool plants will thrive in shade, and waterlilies, the glory of most people's pools, really require maximum exposure to sunlight every day if they are to flower well.

The second consideration must be to find a position well away from deciduous trees. This does not simply mean somewhere that is not overhung by trees, for a pool seems to act like a magnet for leaves that are blown around the garden, and it really is worth looking to see if your chosen spot is one where eddies occur and leaves collect. It will be a constant frustration if you have to net the pool every autumn to remove them.

You should also choose a level site. The top of a slope is acceptable, but if you site the pool on a terrace half-way down a slope or, worse still, at the bottom of a slope, rain run-off will constantly pour into the pool, causing it to overflow and the ground around it to become waterlogged. In such a situation, too, any chemicals that you use in the rest of the garden will be washed down into the pool, to the detriment of the wildlife.

What is the smallest possible size for a pool?

All things considered, the larger the pool, the easier it is to achieve a balance between the plants, fish and other life within it, and anything smaller than about 2 x 1m (6 x 3ft) will create so many problems that it will not be worth the trouble. By the time you have allowed for marginal shallows into which planting baskets can be placed, there will be insufficient water of sufficient depth not to freeze solid in winter, and the pool will not, therefore, be able to maintain a fish population all year round.

If, however, you are prepared to have a very few, very small plants, the tub garden is a possible alternative. Wooden half-barrels are widely available at garden centres, and when they have been thoroughly scrubbed inside, they may either be sunk to the rim in soil or used as a free-standing water feature. If the barrel has been allowed to dry out, it will leak like a sieve for a while but should seal itself tightly as the wood swells again. Do choose a real half-barrel; those made up as plant containers will never be sufficiently watertight.

When the half-barrel is full of water, you will be able to grow a few of the smaller water plants, including miniature waterlilies, such as *Nymphaea* 'Pygmaea Helvola' (yellow flowers) and *N. tetragona* (white flowers). Plant them in plastic containers, covering the soil with gravel. Remember to add half a dozen bunches of submerged oxygenating plants, such as *Ceratophyllum demersum* (hornwort), and you will find that a pair of small fish and a few water snails should live satisfactorily in such a tub garden.

ABOVE: A very attractive small water garden can be created in a tub; but don't over-plant it.

What is the best time of year to create a new pool?

Bear in mind that a pool, if it is built properly, will not be created overnight, and you should plan the work in stages over a period of weeks or even months.

Ideally, work should begin in autumn with the major excavation of the hole and the redistribution of the soil that you remove. You may well want to use the soil to create raised areas, either close to the pool itself or elsewhere in your garden, and the great advantage of an autumn start is that the soil – both in the hole and in the heaps – can be allowed to settle. Continue in mild weather in early spring with the installation of the pool liner and filling with water. This, in turn, should be allowed to settle for several weeks before the plants and, later still, fish are introduced in early summer.

tip

Excavating a pool

It is all too easy to describe excavating the pool as but one step in creating a pool. In fact, it is the most difficult and most time-consuming part of the entire operation and should not be undertaken lightly. Before you begin, decide if you need some form of mechanical help with the excavation process. If so, will access be a problem? It would be sensible to dig a trial trench to about 45cm (18in) deep across the proposed site to make sure that you will be able to excavate to sufficient depth. Next, think about where the spoil from the excavation will go. It is likely that a pool of any size is going to involve the removal of far more soil than can be accommodated simply by adding a layer to your existing beds and borders. Also, of course, you will probably be removing poor quality subsoil after the topsoil has been removed, and you will not want to add this to your borders. What arrangements, if any, do you need to make for the removal of the waste?

RIGHT: Don't try to skimp on the hard work and make your pool too shallow.

Should I put the fish into my pool at the same time as the plants?

It is better to wait for three or four weeks after planting before fish are introduced. This will give the plants an opportunity to become established and give the water time to settle after the inevitable disturbance that adding plants involves.

Remember to place grit over the soil in the planting baskets, otherwise the fish will simply churn the soil up and probably uproot the plants in the process.

INSTALLING A POND
1 Mark out the perimeter of the pool. The easiest way to 'draw' curves is with a hosepipe on a warm day when the hose is flexible.
2 Excavate the hole to the required depth (at least 45cm/18in), leaving ledges for marginal plants.
3 Put sand or a fibre liner in the pool and then lay the butyl liner on top (allowing plenty of overlap at the edges). Slowly fill with water.

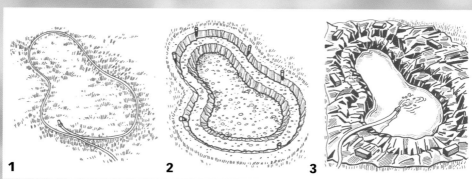

1   2   3

Is there any way that I can have a water feature even though my garden is too small for a pool?

A wall-mounted fountain, a pebble pool or a millstone pond are water features that take up minimal space and that use a small tank of water that is constantly recycled. Kits are now obtainable, including, if that is your choice, replica millstones, and these make the installation of all these features relatively simple. All use low-voltage electricity supplies. A cautionary note relates to wall fountains: do not try to install one on the side of your house and be aware that, in order to fit it, you must own and have access to both sides of the wall.

ABOVE: Even without a proper, full-sized garden pool it's still possible to create an attractive water feature.

How should I prepare the site for a pool?

Whether you use a preformed pool or a flexible liner, the overall principles are similar.

If you are using a preformed pool liner lay the liner on the ground and mark out the shape with pegs or with a flexible hosepipe, allowing about 25–30cm (10–12in) more all round than the size of the liner itself. Dig out a hole to the depth of the liner, plus about 5–7.5cm (2–3in), taking account of any ledges or ridges within the liner. Remove all stones. Lay sand in the bottom of the hole to a depth of about 5–7.5cm (2–3in) to take up the additional depth, and carefully place the liner in position so that the lip of the liner is flush with the surrounding soil surface. Check carefully at this stage that the liner is level in all directions, and then pour in more sand to fill the gap between the sides of the liner and the sides of the hole. Make an edging with regular stone slabs to create a formal pool, or irregularly arranged ones for a semi-natural planting. Mortar the edging stones in position for safety.

If you are using a flexible butyl liner mark out the shape of your pool on the ground; again, you will find that using a hosepipe is the easiest way to 'draw' curves. Measure a rectangle that will accommodate the size and shape you have drawn and add approximately twice the depth to both the width and the length, then add on about 30cm (12in) to both dimensions to give the size of sheet that you require.

Dig the hole for the pool. Remember to create ledges of different depths on which planting baskets will stand and make a shallow shelf, approximately 20cm (8in) wide, all around the edge for marginal plants. Use a spirit level to check that the edge of the pool is level in all directions. Remove all stones and, to protect the butyl, line the hole with proprietary matting or a layer of sand. Lay the butyl sheet across the hole, temporarily anchoring it with rocks or bricks, and then slowly begin to add water from a hosepipe into the centre. The liner will gradually stretch to fill the contours of the pool, and you will need to move the anchoring rocks to accommodate this. Once the pool is almost full, trim the liner to give an overlap all round of about 20cm (8in) and mortar slabs or bricks on this in the usual way for a formal pool or more irregular rocks for an informal one. Soil can be packed against the outside of the rocks to create a planting area near to an informal pool or a bog garden can be created alongside it.

Electricity in the garden

If you are planning any water feature that involves the use of electricity – from a submersible pump to lighting – seek the advice and help of an experienced and qualified electrician.

Which plants are suitable for growing in the water at the edge of my pond?

There is a huge number of these plants, which are called marginals. Their roots must be constantly wet, but the bulk of the plant is held erect above the water, much like a normal herbaceous perennial. As with water plants, some are very vigorous, and although they can be kept in check by regular division in a large water garden, they can cause serious problems in small pools. Some also have sharp, almost needle-like rhizomes, which can easily penetrate a flexible pool liner and cause leaks. I have selected those that are most amenable to being grown in smaller pools:

* *Calla palustris* (bog arum)
* *Caltha palustris* (kingcup, marsh marigold)
* *Cotula coronopifolia* (brass buttons)
* *Equisetum hyemale* (scouring rush)
* *Houttuynia cordata* 'Chameleon'
* *Iris ensata* (Japanese water iris); *I. laevigata* (water iris), *I. versicolor* (blue flag)
* *Ranunculus flammula* (lesser spearwort)
* *Zantedeschia aethiopica* (arum lily)

RIGHT: Zantedeschias make wonderful marginal plants in milder areas.

tip

Choosing plants for a bog garden

There is an enormous range of plants that will thrive in a bog garden, including many, such as bergenias, hostas and astilbes, that are found in most gardens. Take the opportunity that a bog garden provides to grow some of the more unusual plants that will thrive in these conditions.

* *Arisaema triphyllum* (Jack-in-the-pulpit)
* *Arum italicum* subsp. *italicum* 'Marmoratum' (syn. *A. italicum* 'Pictum')
* *Cimicifuga racemosa* (black snake root)
* *Darmera peltata* (syn. *Peltiphyllum peltatum*)
* *Heloniopsis orientalis*
* *Parochetus communis*
* *Potentilla palustris* (syn. *Comarum palustre*; marsh cinquefoil)
* *Primula florindae* (giant cowslip)
* *Saururus cernuus* (lizard's tail, swamp lily)
* *Tricyrtis hirta* var. *alba* (white toad lily)

RIGHT: Candelabra primulas and irises are among the many choice plants for a bog garden.

BELOW: The waterlily variety 'Gladstoneana' combines fragrant double flowers with lovely dark-coloured foliage.

I have been told that my pool needs oxygenating plants. What should I choose?

Your pool certainly needs oxygen in order for fish and plants to thrive. Whether it needs oxygenating plants depends on whether there is a fountain, for the constant running of a moderately large fountain perfectly adequately oxygenates the water. In still pools, however, or those with a very tiny or intermittently operated fountain, submerged plants that give off oxygen from their leaves have an important role to play. The most effective, listed here, have masses of very small leaves:

- *Ceratophyllum demersum* (hornwort)
- *Elodea canadensis* (Canadian pondweed)
- *Lobelia dortmanna* (water lobelia)
- *Myriophyllum spicatum* and *M. verticillatum* (water milfoil)

Can you suggest some easy-to-grow water plants?

Water plants are those that grow entirely within the pond itself, either rooted in the bottom or floating freely. The floating types must be selected with especial care because many are so vigorous that in countries with warmer climates it is illegal to grow some species for fear that they will invade natural water courses and obstruct them. I would recommend the following:

Floating plants

- *Eichhornia crassipes* (water hyacinth)
- *Hottonia palustris* (water violet)
- *Hydrocharis morsus-ranae* (frogbit)
- *Stratiotes aloides* (water soldier)
- *Trapa natans* (water caltrop, water chestnut)
- *Utricularia vulgaris* (bladderwort)

Water plants

- *Aponogeton distachyos* (Cape pondweed, water hawthorn)
- *Hippuris vulgaris* (mare's tail)
- *Nymphaea* cvs. (waterlily)
- *Nymphoides peltata* (water fringe, yellow floating heart)
- *Orontium aquaticum* (golden club)
- *Persicaria amphibia* (willow grass)

I like the idea of a bog garden. How should I set about establishing one in my garden?

You should begin with a low-lying area of your garden and then devise a way of keeping the soil constantly moist but not stagnant. The best way is to follow the guidelines for creating a pool with a flexible butyl rubber liner (see page 105). Do not add protective matting and instead of filling the liner with water, punch a series of small holes in it and then fill the hollow with good quality soil. One way to help keep it moist is to direct the downpipe from the roof of a greenhouse or other outbuilding to discharge into the liner. In spells of prolonged hot, dry weather, you will have to water the plants regularly and thoroughly.

Do I need to smash the ice on my pool in the winter?

No, definitely not. Smashing the ice will set up shock waves in the water that can harm or even kill any fish in the pool. It is important, however, not to leave the pool surface frozen over because this prevents the exchange of gases and leads to the build-up of noxious ones within the water. The most satisfactory way to keep at least part of the pool surface free from ice is with a small, floating, low-voltage pool heater or, if you have one, by keeping the fountain running constantly. I do not advocate floating rubber balls in the water, partly because they look so unattractive and partly because they do not work. If all else fails, slowly pour a kettle full of hot water into a corner of the pool, taking care that you do not damage any dormant plants.

ABOVE: If ice is allowed to form, and remain, on your pool, the fish and plant life will inevitably suffer.

How frequently should I clean out my garden pool?

Almost never. As long as the plants and fish in your pool are thriving and the whole looks – and smells – appealing there is no need to clean it out. These are all signs that a correct balance between the various components has been achieved. The only reason for wanting or needing to clean out a pool, apart from the need to attend to 'mechanical' failures such as leaks, is if there has been an abnormal build-up of putrefying organic matter in the bottom and the consequent production of noxious and harmful gases.

Paying regular attention to removing deciduous leaves and dividing marginal plants and submerged aquatics should help to maintain a healthy balance.

Cleaning a pool
If it becomes necessary to empty a pool for any reason, try to undertake the work in spring so that the plants have the remainder of the year to re-establish themselves. Fish should be placed in a holding tank containing water from the pre-cleaned pool while you work.

How can I stop the water in my pool turning green and murky?

I am afraid that it is impossible to stop pool water turning green. The murkiness is caused by the proliferation of single-celled green algae. The process is sometimes called blooming, and it happens most commonly soon after a new pool has been filled with water. Before long, the water clears again as the population of algae returns to a normal level. Blooming occasionally occurs during hot summer weather, but the problem will always disappear with the onset of the first frosts in autumn. I am among those who believe that using tapwater to fill or top up the pool encourages the development of algal growth; but I am also realistic enough to know that this is unavoidable since there simply isn't enough rainwater.

I have a problem in my garden pool with blanketweed. How can I control it without harming the inhabitants of the pool?

The factors that encourage blanketweed are similar to those that encourage green murky water (see above). This is, as you might expect, because both are types of algae, but blanketweed is multicellular and filamentous instead of single-celled. If blanketweed is allowed to grow unchecked it will very soon swamp all plant life in the pool and lead to serious problems. Chemicals are available to control blanketweed, but I would not recommend them because they result in the different problem of dead blanketweed, which accumulates on the bottom of the pool and rots. Much the best option is to pull it out, which you can easily do by hand or, failing that, with a forked stick. Rafts of barley or lavender straw placed in the water are also effective at diminishing the growth of blanketweed.

RIGHT: Blanketweed is almost certain to appear in your pool at some stage.

Lawns

Do you prefer seed or turf for creating a new lawn?

I would always recommend turf, but only if cost is not a consideration. As long as you buy top-quality, purpose-grown turf, you will have an instant lawn. But it will be much more expensive than seed, and gardeners with a large area to lay are likely to find the cost prohibitive.

The soil preparation is the same for both (see page 113), and laying turf is relatively straightforward, if hard work, because turves are very heavy. Even with modern sprinkler devices, however, it isn't easy to sow lawn seed uniformly and even harder to make sure that it is lightly covered with soil after sowing but not buried deeply. Both require regular watering – but not flooding – afterwards. Newly laid turf may be walked on after about ten days and lightly mown (with a rotary mower only) after about two more weeks. A newly seeded lawn shouldn't be walked on for about two months and should not be mown for about one month more, again with a rotary mower. One of the biggest problems with a sown lawn is that there are no weed-killers available for you to use until the grass is really growing well, by which time perennial weeds may also have become well established.

Choosing a lawn seed

An ornamental lawn should be sown with fine-leaved grasses, such as *Festuca* spp. (fescue) and *Agrostis* spp. (bent). A lawn that is going to receive anything more than light wear should be sown with coarse-leaved grasses, such as *Lolium perenne* (perennial rye grass), *Cynosurus cristatus* (crested dog's tail) and *Poa* spp. (meadow grass).

What is rye grass and why do some lawn seed mixtures contain it?

Rye is a type of grass with particularly tough leaves. It has been used to breed a range of grasses with different growth rates and characteristics but all with the same feature of being damaged much less when trampled than some of the other lawn grass species, like fescues, which have thinner, more delicate foliage. Rye grasses are incorporated in seed mixtures and grown turf that is to withstand considerable wear and tear – that is, grass that will be subject to normal domestic use. Any lawn that will be walked on or played on, rather than merely looked at, should contain some rye grass. The modern rye grasses are much less coarse in appearance than the older types, and a hard-wearing lawn need no longer look significantly rough.

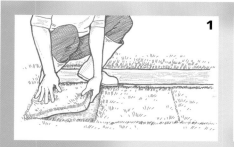

LAYING TURF
1 Stand on a wooden board and lay the turves offset from each other, like bricks.
2 Don't leave a small piece of turf at the end of a row or it will fray. Instead, pull a large piece to the edge and slot the small piece in behind it.

ABOVE: In the right conditions camomile will create a lush green carpet, but don't confuse it with a real lawn.

Is it really possible to make lawns from plants other than grass?

It depends on your definition of a lawn. It is certainly possible to clothe an area with very low-growing, mat-forming plants that are, in effect, very close ground cover. It is also possible to choose plants that will tolerate a degree of being walked on, but you will not be able to replicate the hard-wearing characteristics of grass and nor will you be able to mow it properly. Probably the toughest and prettiest plants to use are the prostrate types of *Thymus* spp. (thyme), such as *T. serpyllum*, *T. polytrichus* subsp. *britannicus* (syn. *T. praecox* subsp. *arcticus*), *T. caespitosus* and *T.* 'Doone Valley'.

The plant that everyone asks about and that certainly has the closest superficial resemblance to a real lawn is camomile. If you use the non-flowering cultivar *Chamaemelum nobile* 'Treneague' you will have a rather attractive feature for a small area. Remember, however, that it will succeed only on a light soil and in a sunny position and that all weeds (including weed grass) must be removed by hand.

I would like to create a wildflower meadow. How should I set about it?

The most important rule is not to leave your lawn to grow long. If you do this, you will end up with long grass but no wildflowers. You need to start from scratch with a special meadow seed mixture, and, if you are going to do it properly, you will need an area not much less than 100 square metres (more than 1000 square feet). If fertilizer has previously been applied to the area, grasses and some of the clovers and vetches present in the meadow mixture will proliferate at the expense of the others. The most effective way to suppress them is to augment the seed mixture with *Rhinanthus minor* (yellow rattle, hay rattle), a plant that is partially parasitic on grasses.

Sow exactly as for a normal lawn. Then use a rotary mower with a grass collector in the first season. Set the blades high – about 7.5cm (3in) – and cut the new meadow throughout the first summer. Thereafter, leave the cutting until as late in the summer as you can. You will probably find that the rotary mower cannot cope then, so you must use either a traditional scythe or a strimmer. Allow the hay to lie while the seeds are shed (turn it once or twice) and use a lawn or hay rake to remove the cut grass after a few days.

RIGHT: Wildflower meadows sound wonderful in theory but are difficult to create successfully.

My lawn is all humps and hollows. How can I remove them?

You must tackle the humps and hollows one by one, and, if you work carefully, it should be possible to flatten even the most undulating lawn in time. Identify individual humps and hollows and cut through the turf on each in an H shape, using a lawn-edging tool. Peel back the turf, as if it were carpet, from the cuts and then either remove or add soil as appropriate. If you are adding soil to a hollow, create a slightly raised area because it will settle in time. As you roll back the turf, you may need to trim off or add small pieces of turf to create a good fit.

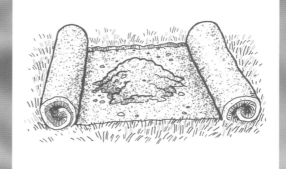

PATCHING AND LEVELLING
Cut an H-shape in the turf and peel back the sides. Then use sieved soil (with no clods or stones) to fill the hollow. Alternatively, carefully scrape away soil to remove humps.

ABOVE: A lawn is really only as good as the care and attention you put into the initial preparation of the site.

What advice can you give on preparing a site for a new lawn?

Work as long in advance as possible and be as thorough as possible. In an ideal world, you would begin to prepare the site a year in advance, giving yourself one summer to apply the translocated weedkiller glyphosate (which works well only in warm weather) to make completely sure that you have removed all perennial weeds.

The site need not be flat. A gentle slope is both acceptable and in some respects aesthetically desirable, but because it is time-consuming to remove extensive humps and hollows once a lawn is established (see opposite), care in grading the site to obtain a flat or uniformly sloping surface beforehand will pay dividends many times over. After grading, the whole site must be levelled and firmed. The most effective tool for levelling and removing stones and clods of soil is the spring-tine lawn rake. It is important to rake alternately in two directions, at right angles to each other, or you may introduce and accentuate rather than diminish any humps and hollows. Firming is done most easily by carefully treading. Do not, whatever you do, use a roller, which will simply create humps and hollows. About a week before you lay the lawn, scatter autumn lawn fertilizer over the area; use the same fertilizer even if you are doing the job in spring because it is important to use a blend with a relatively low nitrogen content.

Yes, if you scatter it lightly over the surface in the autumn, preferably after the lawn has been spiked. It will be pulled down into the soil by worms and will help to improve the soil's structure. But do not scatter it so thickly that the grass beneath turns yellow before the worms have done their work.

LEFT: The garden in winter has a special charm, but you shouldn't walk on the frozen lawn in order to admire it.

How can I do winter lawn care when you are supposed not to walk on it in winter?

I think you may be confusing two pieces of advice. There are two reasons people are advised not to walk on the lawn in winter. When the grass is frozen, you will break the grass leaves, which will die and later turn brown, leaving unsightly footprints that persist until growth begins again in the spring. So try to avoid walking on the grass in frosty weather. The second reason is the more general advice to walk on wet, winter lawns as infrequently as possible because you will create muddy patches, which may then be invaded by weeds.

Clearly, to carry out winter care, such as raking, you will have to walk on the lawn; but keep it to the minimum.

Spiking is very hard work. Is it worthwhile?

It is if you do it properly. Use a hollow-tine spiking tool, which removes a core of soil. Sand or well-sieved compost (see opposite) to which fertilizer has been added may then be brushed into the holes to improve drainage and aeration. Spiking with a fork is less valuable, especially on a heavy soil, because the operation of pushing the fork in merely smears and compresses the soil and may, in reality, compound the problem.

RIGHT: With a heavily compacted lawn, you will find it worth your while to hire a powered spiking machine

BELOW: Red thread disease is one of a number of fungal problems that can create brown patches.

Why are there bare patches on my lawn?

There are a number of reasons for bare patches on lawns, and you will need to decide which might be applicable to your own situation before you undertake remedial work.

It is possible that someone has carelessly spilled something on the grass; petrol from a lawnmower is the commonest. If the damage is severe, you should dig out the dead turf and use one of the modern 'lawn repair kits', which contain treated grass seed in an organic growing medium with added fertilizer.

If the soil is very shallow or compacted, it will suffer in periods of drought but you need do nothing and life will return with the rain.

Leatherjackets (the larvae of craneflies or daddy-long-legs) will kill the grass in patches because they feed on the roots. This occurs most often in dry weather and the easiest way to check the cause and also control the pests is to soak the affected patches of the lawn thoroughly and place a plastic sheet over these areas late in the evening. Any larvae in the soil will work their way to the surface where they can be swept up in the morning.

Some types of root-attacking lawn fungi can cause brown patches, usually when spring or summer lawn feed has been used too late in the year and has promoted soft, lush growth in winter. Apply feed at the appropriate time of year, and the problem should resolve itself.

How can I restore the lawn after a summer of children's games and family activity?

Here is my five-point plan for lawn revival. Try to carry out as many of these tasks as you can:

* Apply lawn sand or proprietary moss killer.
* Scarify to remove dead moss and thatch.
* Go over the surface with a hollow-tine spiking tool (see page 115).
* Apply autumn lawn fertilizer.
* Mow during the winter whenever the weather is mild and the grass is growing, using a rotary mower with the blades set as high as possible; this will also remove twigs and other debris.

ABOVE: A spring lawn rake will remove some of the thatch of dead grass and moss.

RIGHT: It is almost impossible permanently to eradicate fairy rings from the lawn.

How can I eradicate the toadstools from my lawn?

You cannot, not permanently, but there is no need to worry unduly. Isolated toadstools or small groups of toadstools will have no effect at all on the growth of the grass because they will be growing and feeding on organic matter in the soil.

More or less circular groups of toadstools, usually called fairy rings, do have some effect on grass growth, however. If you look carefully, you will see an outer ring of dark, rather lush grass, then a ring of toadstools and, in the centre, a ring of brown, dead grass. Remove the fungi as soon as you see them to prevent the spores from spreading. The dead area should be raked out, the soil spiked, re-sown or re-turfed and given additional fertilizer in the following season. Because the fungi causing the fairy ring often develop on buried woody material, it is worth digging down to remove the material.

How can I have a good lawn without removing the daisies?

You must either hand weed to remove only the other types of weed and not the daisies or apply a lawn weedkiller extremely carefully. If the daises are scattered more or less everywhere, hand weeding is the only real option because there is no weedkiller available that is able to distinguish between daisies and other broad-leaved plants.

ABOVE: Many people like to see daisies on their lawn – which is just as well, as they can be hard to eradicate.

LEFT: White clover is one of the trickiest of the creeping lawn weeds to eradicate.

There are masses of small, creeping weeds in my lawn. How can I get rid of them?

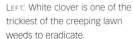

The most common and important small creeping weeds are: *Medicago lupulina* (black medick), *Ranunculus repens* (creeping buttercup), *Convolvulus arvensis* (field bindweed), *Trifolium dubium* (lesser trefoil), *Rumex acetosella* (procumbent yellow sorrel), *Trifolium repens* (white clover) and *Achillea millefolium* (yarrow). The clover-like, yellow-flowered lesser trefoil is an annual; the others are all perennial.

Good lawn management will help to discourage these weeds, although it will not entirely prevent them and certainly will not eradicate them. Feed in spring and autumn with an appropriate fertilizer and never set the mower blades so low that the lawn is shaved. These actions will encourage the grass to grow effectively and compete with the weeds. Use a mower with a collector box so that seedheads and cuttings of the weeds are not spread even further around the lawn.

To eradicate existing weeds, you will need to resort to chemical weed control, and, because this is a lawn, you will need a selective lawn weedkiller. Nevertheless, some lawn weeds are extremely difficult to eradicate, even with chemicals, and I suggest that you ring the changes by using a different weedkiller if the first treatment does not work or works only partially. Different proprietary products contain different blends of chemicals, and some weeds in some places seem to be resistant to one or more of them.

Can you suggest an annual feeding regime for my lawn?

I always recommend that lawns be fed twice a year, in spring and in autumn. It is essential, however, to use fertilizer blends that have been specifically formulated for the two different seasons. The spring fertilizer should have a relatively high nitrogen content in order to boost the grass through the summer growing season. The autumn blend should have proportionately more potash to toughen up the foliage for the winter and also a higher phosphate content to stay in the soil, ready to stimulate root growth in early spring. Follow the manufacturer's recommended application rate.

I do not believe that the so-called 'green-up' feeds, which are used in summer, are worthwhile because their effects are short lived and largely cosmetic, giving a temporary darker colour to the grass.

I want to give my lawn a spring feed. Should I use a liquid or a solid blend?

I prefer a solid or, more accurately, a powder fertilizer blend. Liquid fertilizers in general are best used when plants are growing vigorously in the height of the growing season because they are more rapidly absorbed.

Spring feeds are, however, susceptible to being washed from the soil by heavy rain, and the nitrogen component especially may last only a short time if there are frequent heavy spring showers. Many spring fertilizer mixtures have a weedkiller incorporated in them. This is convenient in so far as it obviates the necessity to carry out two separate operations, but weedkillers do not work well in cool conditions, so you should really wait until late spring before applying them.

One problem with powdered fertilizers is that they are not easy to apply uniformly. For this reason, you will find that a product that has a blue dye added is a great help in enabling you to see exactly where you have applied it. A small wheeled spreader will make life immeasurably easier, too, as well as making the application rate more precise.

RIGHT: A wheeled spreader will enable you to spread lawn fertilizer uniformly and neatly.

I garden organically, but the lawn feeds that I have seen all seem to contain artificial chemicals. Is there anything I can use?

It is true that most of'the popular lawn fertilizer brands are based on artificial chemicals. They tend, for instance, to contain ammonium sulphate as the nitrogen source. Nonetheless, it is now possible to buy lawn fertilizers that, like other garden feeds, are based solely or mainly on organic components. For the organic purist, it is important to distinguish between products that are truly organic – that is, that contain only products of natural origin – and those that are organically based. Because there is no readily available organic source of potash and because a mixture containing only fishmeal, dried blood and bonemeal would be potash deficient, potassium sulphate is often added to produce a more useful blend.

ABOVE: Wait until bulbs die down before applying lawn killer so that the bulbs will not be harmed.

I have planted bulbs in my lawn. Can I use weedkillers on it?

Lawn weedkillers are absorbed through green foliage and will only harm plants that are in active growth, which is one reason they do not work well if they are applied too early in the year. Once the bulbs have died down for the summer, therefore, you need have no fear that they will be damaged if you then apply lawn weedkiller.

What is the best type of lawnmower?

There is no easy answer to this question. I have summarized here the advantages and disadvantages of the main types of mower now available:

ABOVE: A hover rotary mower is useful for rougher grass and for mowing beneath low hanging branches.

MOWER TYPE	ADVANTAGES	DISADVANTAGES
CYLINDER	* Produces stripes and attractive lawn appearance * All models have collectors	* Unsuitable for long, wet grass
WHEELED ROTARY	* Produces moderately attractive lawn appearance * All models have collectors * Larger models can cope with long, wet grass * Large models are uniquely useful for winter use	* Produces imperfect stripes
HOVER ROTARY	* Allows access to difficult places, such as under shrubs * Suitable for slopes and uneven ground * All models are relatively small and lightweight * Some models have collectors	* Does not produce stripes * Gives unattractive lawn appearance * Unsuitable for long, wet grass
POWER TYPE		
MAINS ELECTRICITY		* Low to medium engine power * Limited in operation to cable length from mains * Needs circuit breaker for safe operation
BATTERY		* Small number of models available * Low to medium engine power * Limited in operation to time battery retains charge (usually about 1 hour)
PETROL	* High engine power therefore good for big mowers * Effectively unlimited in range and time	* Weight of engine precludes use with small machines

How good are the electric devices that are available for trimming the edge of lawns?

These machines are not nearly as good as a pair of high quality edging shears, and on irregular edges, they will scalp the turf. I am not at all enthusiastic about them, and nor would I recommend the similar devices that clip on the side of some electric mowers. What has impressed me, however, is the option that is available on some petrol-powered cylinder mowers that makes it possible to remove the cylinder of blades and replace it with a scarifier cartridge.

ABOVE: Nothing produces stripes in a lawn like a powered cylinder mower.

Do you recommend keeping the grass box on the mower?

Yes, I do. I do not subscribe to the theory that returning the mowings directly to the lawn provides any benefit to the grass. If the grass is cut very often – at least twice a week – and the mowings are, therefore, very small, there might be some moisture-retaining, mulching advantage, but there can be few gardeners these days who mow that frequently.

Even rotary and hover mowers are now available with grass-collection boxes, and my advice is to use them. The mowings should, of course, be used in the garden but only after they have been composted.

What is the secret of perfect stripes in a lawn?

You should use a good cylinder mower that has a small roller at the rear. The combination of the blades and the roller pushes the grass forwards, and as the direction of mowing is reversed at the end of each run, the light reflecting differently off the grass blades in consecutive rows gives the effect of stripes.

A rotary mower with a roller will produce stripes of a sort but nothing matches those produced by a cylinder. Mowing twice at right angles will give a more interesting effect, and really adventurous gardeners might like to try mowing in alternate directions in concentric circles to create something even more eye-catching.

Bulbs, corms &
tubers

What is the difference between a bulb, a tuber and a corm – and does it matter?

BELOW: *Allium cristophii* is a bulbous plant that can remain in the ground permanently, without the need to be lifted.

Bulbs (such as those of daffodils and tulips) are swollen buds; tubers are either swollen stems (such as potatoes) or swollen roots (such as dahlias); corms (such as those of gladioli) are swollen stem bases, while rhizomes (such as those of border irises) are swollen underground stems. All these structures have one thing in common: they are food-storage organs and serve to give plants a head-start in the new season. Provided they are of good quality, therefore, you can be almost careless in the way that you treat and plant them, and they will still flower for you in the first year. Their performance in the following years will, however, suffer if you do not treat them carefully (see page 124).

Does the difference matter? Yes it does, in the sense that knowing the type of structure is a pretty good guide to how they should be planted. In general, bulbs, tubers and corms should be planted deeply, and rhizomes more shallowly. The main exceptions among ornamental plants are the bulbs of nerine and *Lilium candidum* (shallow), cyclamen tubers (shallow) and lily-of-the-valley rhizomes (fairly shallow).

Bulbs, corms and tubers to lift each year	Comment
Dahlia cvs.	Lift and store for replanting in spring
Gladiolus cvs.	Lift and store for replanting in spring
Iris danfordiae	Discard; they will not flower reliably after the first year
Narcissus – all cultivars not described as 'good for naturalizing'	Lift and store for replanting in autumn
Tulipa – all large-flowered cvs.	Discard and buy new stock

Is it worth lifting bulbs from the garden every year?

Whether you lift bulbs depends largely on the species, and listed on the left are those that I believe should be lifted each year. This advice is based on the belief that you really do want to obtain the best from the bulbs you buy. You can leave all hardy bulbs in the garden for as long as you like, but the flowering performance of some will decline very steeply after the first year or two. Some types – hybrid lilies and some types of *Allium* especially – will decline after a few years in the garden because of attacks by viruses and slugs and from other causes, but they will last for very many years if grown in large containers.

tip

Buying snowdrops

Although snowdrop bulbs are available in autumn, they can fail to establish. You will have more success if you buy snowdrops from a specialist nursery in spring, when they are 'in the green' – that is, they still have leaves. Plant them in the border to the same depth as before.

How can I have a succession of bulbs right through the year?

A year-round succession can be achieved by a careful choice of varieties and by not filling your available space with too many plants of one type. If you have a massed planting of daffodils, for instance, even with a large number of different cultivars, you will not achieve much more than about two months' worth of flowers. Listed below are my suggestions for some commonly available plants that will give you continuity of flowers through the year.

SPRING

- *Anemone nemorosa* (wood anemone)
- *Bulbocodium vernum* (spring saffron)
- *Chionodoxa* spp. (glory of the snow)
- *Convallaria majalis* (lily-of-the-valley)
- *Corydalis* spp. (spring fumitory)
- *Crocus* spp. and cvs.
- *Erythronium* spp. (dog's tooth violet)
- *Fritillaria* spp.
- *Gagea* spp.
- *Hyacinthoides* spp. (bluebell)
- *Ipheion uniflorum*
- *Leucojum* spp. (snowflake)
- *Muscari* spp. (grape hyacinth)
- *Narcissus* spp. and cvs. (daffodil)
- *Ornithogalum* spp. (star of Bethlehem)
- *Scilla* spp. (squill)
- *Trillium* spp. (wood lily, Trinity flower)
- *Tulipa* spp. and cvs.

SUMMER

- *Agapanthus* spp. (African lily)
- *Allium* spp. (ornamental onion)
- *Alstroemeria* spp. (Peruvian lily)
- *Amaryllis belladonna*
- *Camassia* spp. (quamash)
- *Cardiocrinum* spp. (giant lily)
- *Crinum* spp.
- *Eremurus* spp. (foxtail lily, desert candle)
- *Galtonia* spp.
- *Gladiolus* cvs.
- *Iris* spp. and cvs.
- *Lilium* spp. (lily)
- *Schizostylis coccinea* (Kaffir lily)
- *Zantedeschia* spp. (arum lily)

AUTUMN

- *Colchicum* spp. (autumn crocus, naked ladies)
- *Crocosmia* spp. and cvs. (montbretia)
- *Crocus sativus* (saffron crocus); *C. speciosus*
- *Dahlia* cvs.
- *Cyclamen hederifolium*
- *Nerine* spp.
- *Sternbergia* spp.

WINTER

- *Anemone blanda*
- *Crocus ancyrensis*; *C. laevigatus* 'Fontenayi'
- *Cyclamen coum*
- *Eranthis hyemalis* (winter aconite)
- *Galanthus* spp. (snowdrop)

TOP: *Narcissus poeticus recurvus*, the 'old pheasant's eye' narcissus, is one of the best loved *Narcissus* varieties.

ABOVE: *Tulipa tarda* is an excellent species tulip and naturalizes very readily.

Every time I plant bulbs, they flower well for a year or two, then produce only leaves. What am I doing wrong?

There are two possible reasons: either you have chosen inappropriate types or you have planted and/or cared for them incorrectly.

For growing in the garden you must select bulbs that are hardy and described as good for naturalizing. On page 122 is a list of the species that will not flower reliably or survive *in situ* after the first year. Even with the correct choice of plants, however, failures often occur, most commonly with narcissi. The most likely reasons are:

* The bulbs have been planted too deeply. Remember the maxim of planting with the base of the bulb at a depth equal to about three times its diameter.
* The bulbs have rotted; see guidelines for planting (opposite).
* The bulbs have been attacked by the narcissus fly. To help avoid this, rake some soil over the plants after you have cut down the foliage and old flower stems; otherwise, as they shrivel, a hole develops, which allows the flies to crawl down to the bulbs and lay their eggs.
* You have not allowed the bulbs to renew their food reserves. After flowering, it is most important to allow six weeks before you cut back the foliage and during this time, give several applications of liquid fertilizer.

ABOVE: *Narcissus* 'February Gold' will flower reliably every year but benefits from some feeding as the flowers fade.

I planted masses of crocus corms but hardly any came up. What went wrong?

The explanation is almost certainly small, furry and four-footed. Voles and, to a lesser extent, mice are irresistibly drawn to crocuses, whether they are in the ground or in store. Please do not be tempted to try trapping them; you will catch one every time you put down a trap. It is much better to give the corms some protection when you plant them. Dig planting holes for groups of corms about 1cm (½in) deeper than normal, cover them lightly with soil and then lay fine mesh chicken wire over the top. Cover this with soil in the usual way. It will be a very persistent vole that tries to eat its way through wire netting, but the crocuses will not be troubled and the shoots will find their way upwards in spring.

LEFT: Like other types of crocus, *Crocus kotschyanus* is a magnet for voles and mice.

Can bulbs be grown from seed?

Yes, indeed they can, and many types, such as cyclamen and chionodoxas, will self-seed and spread readily in the garden. If you want to do things in a more controlled way, collect the seed as soon as it is ripe and sow it on the surface of a soil-based seedling compost. Cover lightly with sand and place the seed trays or pots in a cold frame. Germination should take place slowly and erratically during the following year. You should expect to wait for anything between two and seven years (depending on the size of the bulb) before the new plants flower.

LEFT: I always place a layer of sand in the base of the hole before planting bulbs.

How should I prepare the soil before I plant bulbs?

Almost any preparation is more than most people provide. All too often, bulbs are stuffed under grass and into the most improbably awful soil. Above all, it is important not to plant into constantly wet ground. Dig in organic matter well in advance of planting, much as you would when preparing the ground for herbaceous plants. Then, when you are preparing the planting positions, add a layer of horticultural sand to which a little bonemeal has been added in the base of the planting hole. This will improve the drainage immediately beneath the bulbs and help to minimize the likelihood of rotting of the basal plate, the vulnerable area from which the roots develop.

Lilies are very expensive to buy. Is there a simple way to multiply them?

Yes there is, and the main method is called bulb scaling. It is simple to carry out and will cost you nothing, but you won't have plants of flowering size for about four years.

If you look closely at a lily bulb you will see that it consists of a group of thick, overlapping scales, rather like a bloated onion. These are individual leaves, and they can be used to produce new plants. Autumn is the best time for this, during the short period when the bulbs are dormant. Pull two or three scales from each bulb; do not take more than this, or you may weaken the bulb itself. Pop the scales into a plastic bag with some moist sphagnum moss. Tie the bag and leave it in a warm place – an airing cupboard is ideal – and check it regularly. After about five weeks each scale should have formed tiny roots and can be potted up on its own.

As an alternative to scales, try using bulbils. These are the small, dark, bulb-like objects that some types of lily – notably *Lilium lancifolium* (syn. *L. tigrinum*; tiger lily) and *L. bulbiferum* and their hybrids – form on their stems. When the stem is dying at the end of the season, cut it from the plant before the bulbils are shed. Carefully remove the individual bulbils and 'sow' them, just pressed into the surface of a soil-less compost and grow them on. They, too, will take about four years to attain flowering size.

RIGHT: Lilies are ideal bulbs for growing in containers where they will be much more trouble-free.

I think lilies are the most beautiful bulbs, but I have been put off growing them because of the problems that seem to dog them. Have I been unlucky?

I agree that lilies are beautiful, but I do think that they are especially susceptible to a range of problems. In some areas, especially the south of England, the biggest problem now is the lily beetle, a voracious pest with disgusting-looking, slimy larvae. Both adults and larvae eat the foliage and cause serious damage. If spraying with insecticide does not help, I regret that there really is nothing that can be done, because no lily cultivars are resistant to this pest.

Lilies also succumb to a virus that causes a diminution in flowering and a general loss of vigour. I have found that the true species are less likely to succumb than the hybrids. Slugs and fungal diseases can also cause problems, but these can be avoided to a considerable extent by growing your plants in containers rather than in the open ground.

Can you suggest some bulbs that I could plant beneath an ornamental tree?

As with all plantings under trees, try to improve the soil as much as possible by digging in well-rotted organic matter and remember that the plants will need feeding rather more frequently than those in good soil in borders.

The following are my top ten bulbs for this slightly shaded and fairly dry situation:

* *Allium moly* (golden garlic)
* *Convallaria majalis* (lily-of-the-valley)
* *Corydalis* spp.
* *Cyclamen* spp. (especially *C. hederifolium*)
* *Eranthis hyemalis* (winter aconite)
* *Erythronium* spp. (dog's tooth violet)
* *Galanthus* spp. (snowdrop)
* *Hyacinthoides* spp. (bluebell)
* *Leucojum* spp. (snowflake)
* *Muscari* spp. (grape hyacinth)

ABOVE: Muscaris will grow well in the partial shade beneath trees but some types can be invasive.

LEFT: Snake's head fritillaries look wonderful growing in grass, but it must be left unmown.

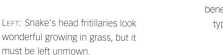

How can I achieve a compromise between naturalizing bulbs in my lawn and keeping the grass in an attractive condition?

The solution lies in recognizing the distinction between a lawn and an area of grass. A lawn is an area that is mown regularly, and this simply isn't conducive to the successful growing of bulbs. As noted on page 124, the foliage must be allowed to remain for six weeks after the flowers have died, and leaving a lawn unmown for six weeks is not good practice.

I have tried to grow snowdrops and early crocuses in grass but without success. What am I doing wrong?

You are probably choosing inappropriate plants. The ability to grow among grass and compete with it requires a plant of considerable vigour. *Galanthus* spp. (snowdrop) just does not have that ability; snowdrops are intolerant of any competition and grow naturally in fairly bare ground, away from other types of plant. Early crocuses, which include several of the small-flowered species and cultivars derived from them, are also incapable of growing in grass, and if you want crocuses naturalized in grass you must choose the large-flowered, later blooming Dutch crocuses, available in their striking shades of blue and purple and in white.

ABOVE: Snowdrops are truly beautiful but grow much better in bare soil than in grass.

Should I cut off the leaves of daffodils and other garden bulbs after they have finished flowering?

Yes, but not immediately. This practice had always been a matter of argument among gardeners until some years ago when careful trials demonstrated that the foliage should be left for a period of six weeks. If the leaves were cut down much before that time, the bulbs would be weakened; if it was left for much longer, there would be no significant advantage and the garden would look unnecessarily untidy.

tip

Crocuses for naturalizing

Not all crocuses are suitable for growing in grass, but the following species and the hybrids derived from them should be reliable: *Crocus biflorus*, *C. chrysanthus*, *C. flavus* (syn. *C. aureus*), *C. nudiflorus*, *C. ochroleucus*, *C. pulchellus*, *C. speciosus* and *C. tommasinianus*. Look out, too, for the Dutch hybrids of *C. vernus*, which flower in late spring and produce leaves before the flowers appear. Among the best known are 'Pickwick' (white and purple), 'Remembrance' (violet), 'Jeanne d'Arc' (white) and *C. x luteus* 'Golden Yellow' (orange).

Was I imagining things, or did I really see snowdrops in summer?

No, you did not see snowdrops but you have probably seen plants with very similar flowers that I think are among the more undervalued garden bulbs. They are called leucojums or snowflakes, and there are three fairly common species from central or southern Europe, each rather confusingly named. *Leucojum vernum*, the so-called spring snowflake, flowers in winter; *L. aestivum*, the summer snowflake, flowers in spring and includes the wonderful tall cultivar 'Gravetye Giant'; and *L. autumnale* flowers in late summer or autumn. They are tolerant of a wide range of conditions but, like snowdrops, tend to be best in slightly moist, heavy soil in light shade.

RIGHT: *Leucojum aestivum* 'Gravetye Giant' is a tall and very beautiful late spring bulb like a huge snowdrop.

ABOVE: Daffodils are simply types of *Narcissus* with elongated trumpets.

What are the differences between daffodils and narcissi?

Botanically, almost none. All are varieties of the genus *Narcissus*, which contains many species and has given rise to thousands of cultivated varieties. They are divided for gardening purposes into about twelve groups, of which the types that gardeners call daffodils are placed in two or three. They are characterized by their markedly elongated trumpets. My top ten garden daffodil cultivars are:

* 'Carlton' – large, pale yellow, frilled cup; to 60cm (24in); mid-spring; good for forcing
* 'Ice Follies' – large, frilled cup, lemon yellow at first, later off-white, cream-white petals; to 40cm (16in); mid-spring
* 'King Alfred' – smooth, broad, golden-yellow petals; to 45cm (18in); I think the best large golden daffodil for naturalizing
* 'Mount Hood' – cream-white trumpet, off-white, overlapping petals; to 45cm (18in); mid-spring; the finest white daffodil
* 'Professor Einstein' – large, frilled, orange cup, white petals; to 60cm (24in); early spring; eye-catching

* 'Rijnveld's Early Sensation' – large, yellow flowers, 9cm (3½in) across; 25–50cm (10–20in); very early
* 'Salmon Trout' – large, buff-yellow cup, white petals; to 60cm (24in); mid-spring
* 'Salome' – large, pink-orange cup, waxy pure white or cream petals; 45cm (18in); mid-spring; the best pink
* Spellbinder' – sulphur yellow trumpet fading to cream, white-green mouth; 50cm (20in); mid-spring
* 'W.P. Milner' – pendent, pale cream-yellow trumpet, forward-pointing cream petals, 23cm (9in); early to mid-spring

ABOVE: The pendulous forms of *Begonia* x *tuberhybrida* make excellent container plants.

I like growing tuberous begonias. What is the best way to treat them after the leaves and stems die down?

There are numerous groups of tuberous begonias, ranging from the small, rather dainty trailing forms for hanging baskets, through various singles and double, camellia-flowered and frilled forms, to the familiar enormous, blowsy types in vibrant colours. They are commonly grown in pots and can be saved for next year after the foliage has died down.

When I have grown a plant in an individual pot I don't remove the tuber from the compost but simply lay the whole thing on its side under the greenhouse bench. Tubers in beds and outdoor containers must, of course, be lifted, carefully dried off and then stored over winter in a frost-free place in boxes of old, dry, soil-less compost. Always dust the tubers with sulphur before storage to protect them from fungal decay.

To start them into growth again, lay the tubers, concave side upwards, in seed trays of soil-less compost in a light, fairly warm place. As soon as growth starts, transfer them to pots of about 15cm (6in) diameter. They will need to be hardened off in the usual way before being planted outside, and you will almost certainly find that the large-flowered doubles will need some staking as support.

I always lose my dahlia tubers over winter. Is there a foolproof way of keeping them?

Once the first frosts have blackened dahlia foliage, cut down the stems to leave about 10cm (4in) above ground level and then lift the tubers carefully with a fork. Use a small cane to poke away the soil between each and then store the whole mass upside down in an airy and frost-free place for a week or so to dry. Lightly dust the tubers with sulphur and wrap each clump individually in an envelope made from a whole copy of a broadsheet newspaper. Leave the envelope open at the top and pack them, open end uppermost, in a cardboard box, which must be kept in a frost-free place. In early spring, unpack them, cut away any dead or damaged parts and place them in the greenhouse to start into growth ready for cuttings to be taken.

I can't get my crown imperials to flower a second time. Is there something I can do?

Fritillaria imperialis (crown imperial) is one of the most majestic of garden flowers and makes a very welcome contrast in shape and structure from the other early-season bulbs. The normal colour is brick red, but a slightly lower-growing, yellow-flowered form is also obtainable.

Your experience is not unusual. These plants flower in the first season, then take a break and gradually return to regular flowering over a period of two or three years. They do not respond well to being moved, again tending to stop flowering for a few years, so it is worth choosing your position for them carefully and then leaving them to settle down.

ABOVE: Crown imperials must be left undisturbed if they are to continue flowering reliably.

Why did the bulbs we planted in our tubs rot before flowering?

The bulbs probably rotted because there was inadequate drainage in the container and/or you did not use a free-draining, open-textured compost. When I am planting in a large tub or similar container, I quarter fill it with broken rocks, crocks and similar matter to give very free drainage at the base, and then top up with compost. This is more economical, too.

LEFT: Many bulbs make excellent container plants but don't forget that they must have good drainage.

Pruning

Do you prefer anvil- or scissor-style pruners – and why?

I use both types of pruner but to carry out different tasks. If you want to buy only one pair, I suggest that you choose the anvil pattern. Scissor or, as they are often called, by-pass secateurs or pruners have two blades, which slide against each other, scissor fashion. They will slice through fairly soft stems to give a clean cut with no ragged edges. On hard, woody branches, however, they are less efficient, and there is always a temptation to twist them to gain a better cut. This will put the blades out of alignment, and it is here that anvil-action pruners come into their own. They are more robust and have one cutting blade, which operates against a flat surface.

Both types of pruner are available in different sizes, and the manufacturers will indicate on the packaging the maximum thickness of stem that can be cut by each size of pruner. It is very important not to exceed this or you will certainly cause damage. Always buy the best quality that you can afford; cheap, badly made pruners can harm shrubs.

Should I paint the pruning cuts after I have pruned my trees and shrubs?

No; this is now recognized to be bad practice. If you look at some older books on gardening, you will see the recommendation that you paint pruning cuts with bitumen or a fungicide-containing preparation. The idea was to prevent decay fungi from entering through the wound. It is now known, however, that this prevents the natural healing processes in the tree from functioning properly.

ABOVE: By-pass pruners are good for softer stems but can be damaged on woody ones.

When should I use loppers and when is it better to use a pruning saw?

Use loppers when branches are too thick to be cut with pruners; use a curved pruning saw when the branches are too thick to be cut with loppers.

When you are using a pruning saw, bear in mind that it is operated in a rather special way. First, you cut on the pull stroke, not the push stroke as with a conventional saw. Second, if you are removing a horizontal branch, you will first need to make a cut halfway through on the underside so that the wood does not split and tear as the branch falls under its own weight.

While I am on the subject of saws, may I put in a plea for gardeners not to use chain saws. These are exceedingly dangerous pieces of equipment, and if they are operated without proper training and instruction in their correct maintenance and use, dreadful accidents can happen.

ABOVE: Long-handled pruners are useful if you have larger trees to deal with.

ABOVE: A powered strimmer is of limited value in rougher parts of the garden but won't give a neat finish.

I strim down ground-cover shrubs instead of pruning them. Will it do any harm?

I have mixed feelings about this. The answer to the question really depends on how shrubby the ground cover is. I use a strimmer for ground-cover plants that are truly semi-herbaceous. *Vinca* spp. (periwinkle) and *Rubus tricolor*, for example, have fairly soft, pliable stems, and strimming cuts through them neatly and stimulates new growth. With tougher and more shrubby plants, like cotoneasters, however, I feel that even with a powerful metal-bladed strimmer (a nylon strimmer just could not cope), the frayed tissue that results can lead to die-back and also looks most unattractive. I would, incidentally, use a similar argument against careless and coarse rose pruning (see page 137).

I have read that cutting off branches flush with the trunk is bad practice but the book didn't say why. Can you explain the reason?

Rather like the advice about applying bitumen or something similar to pruning cuts, this is an old gardening practice that modern research has shown to be unsound.

It is now known that when a tree is damaged in some way, whether accidentally or by a deliberate pruning cut, special processes within its tissues operate to prevent the penetration of decay-causing fungi. The tree produces 'barriers' within the tissues in which resins and other chemicals block the advance of any decay. These defence mechanisms operate mainly in the swollen region at the base of a branch, called the collar. If you saw off a branch flush with the trunk, you will cut away the collar, thereby removing the capacity of the tree to protect itself, and decay will almost certainly enter the wood.

ABOVE: A correctly trimmed branch; cutting into the basal collar harms the tree's natural healing processes.

tip

Summer pruning

Shrubs that flower in spring generally bear the blooms on the previous year's growth, and to encourage the plants to develop strong, new growth they should be pruned after flowering. Among the most widely grown shrubs in this group are:

Buddleja alternifolia; *Chaenomeles* spp. (flowering quince); deciduous species of *Cotoneaster*; *Deutzia* spp.; *Exochorda* spp. (pearl bush); *Jasminum humile* (yellow jasmine); *Kolkwitzia amabilis* (beauty bush); *Magnolia soulangeana* and *M. stellata* (star magnolia); *Philadelphus* spp. (mock orange); *Photinia villsa*; *Ribes sanguineum* (flowering currant); *Spiraea* 'Arguta' (bridal wreath), *S. prunifolia* and *S. thunbergii*; *Stephanandra* spp.; *Syringa* spp. (lilac); and *Weigela* spp.

LEFT: There are many beautiful varieties of *Philadelphus* including several double-flowered forms.

Why shouldn't plums be pruned in autumn – or is this a gardening myth?

No, it certainly isn't a myth. It is, in fact, a means of protecting plums from a very serious disease called silver leaf. This is a fungal infection that affects many different tree species but is especially serious on plums, the popular cultivar 'Victoria' most of all.

The infection takes its name from the silver appearance of the foliage, but its more serious consequences are extensive dying back of the branches and a huge reduction in fruiting. The disease is caused by a fungus that is spread by spores produced in autumn and winter. If these land on exposed wood, they germinate and infect the tree. For this reason, plums should not be pruned in autumn and winter. By pruning in late spring, the pruning cuts are given time to heal before the spores are available.

Will pruning really bring decrepit old shrubs back to life?

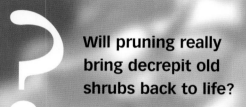

If the plants are 'decrepit' simply through being overgrown and misshapen, the answer is yes. If, however, it is a consequence of being overgrown and neglected, diseased or very seriously weakened, the answer is probably no.

If a shrub is relatively common and of no great aesthetic merit, it is generally more sensible to replace it with a new one. If it is rare, has great sentimental value or is large and in an important position in relation to the rest of the garden, a gradual process of rejuvenation is justified. Do not undertake severe pruning all at once. Instead, spread the work over two or even three years.

ABOVE: Silver leaf disease is aptly named; air in the leaf tissues gives the silvering effect.

Why is it that some shrubs need pruning and some do not?

This is not an easy question to answer because, of course, no shrub needs pruning in the sense that it could not survive without it. If this were true, they would not exist in the wild where gardeners never interfere with them. In the garden some shrubs will flower or otherwise perform below expectations if they are not pruned, but the only common flowering shrubs that would be seriously unattractive without pruning are modern bush roses. All others will flower and retain a reasonably attractive shape with little or no attention; they will simply be neater and tidier if they have some.

Do not forget that pruning isn't only applied to flowering shrubs. Hedge clipping is no less a form of pruning, and without it hedges would completely fail in their purpose.

The thornless variety *R.* 'Zephirine Drouhin' is a popular, though mildew-prone, climber.

Choosing a climbing rose

One of the most often-heard complaints about modern roses is that they lack fragrance. Here are some not-too-vigorous climbers that are strongly scented:

* 'Alister Stella Gray' (syn. 'Golden Rambler') – yellow flowers fading to white; to 5m (16ft)
* 'Climbing Ena Harkness' – double, crimson flowers; to 5m (16ft)
* 'Climbing Lady Hillingdon' – semi-double to double, yellow flowers; to 5m (16ft)
* 'Compassion' (syn. 'Belle de Londres') – double, pink-apricot flowers; to 3m (10ft)
* 'Meg' – semi-double, pink-apricot flowers; to 4m (13ft)
* 'Madame Alfred Carrière' – pale pink to white flowers; to 3m (10ft)
* 'New Dawn' – pale pink flowers; to 3m (10ft)
* 'Paul's Lemon Pillar' (syn. 'Lemon Pillar') – double, white flowers; to 4m (13ft)
* 'Schoolgirl' – apricot-coloured flowers; to 3m (10ft)
* 'Zéphirine Drouhin' – deep pink flowers; to 3m (10ft)

I have a very rampant climbing rose. What is the best way to prune it?

If the plant is rampant to the extent that it has far outgrown its allotted place, you should ask yourself if it is the right rose for its position. Any plant, whether it is a climbing rose or something else, that has to be drastically pruned each year simply to keep it within reasonable bounds is probably an inappropriate choice for its position.

If the plant has simply become unkempt, however, you must first identify a main 'framework' for the plant – that is, the main stem and branches that create the overall shape – and make sure that this is well secured to its support. Next cut back all side-shoots to within about 5cm (2in) of their bases. The best time to do this is in spring so that, during the following season, new growth and new flowering shoots will arise. Repeat the process routinely each year thereafter. You will probably find that new main shoots will develop from the base and, one by one, these should be trained in to replace any very old and woody growths.

Is dead-heading roses really as important as experts claim?

If you want your plants to look tidy, dead-heading is essential, but the practice has other real benefits too, and these are often overlooked. By removing the dead flower heads, you are removing a potential starting point for fungal disease to set in, disease that could spread down the shoot and cause some die-back. This is especially likely to happen in damp, warm weather when mould growth on the dead flowerhead may be considerable.

Dead-heading is also important in encouraging the plant to produce more flowers. As with all pruning, removing the end of a shoot will stimulate new buds to develop further down.

There is one exception to the need for dead-heading, however. Some shrub roses – many of the rugosa roses and some of the species, for instance – produce very attractive autumn fruits (hips). If you dead-head these roses, there will be no possibility of the fruits forming.

ABOVE: Carelessly leaving pruning stubs can allow dieback disease to set in.

I've read that roses can be pruned quite easily with hedge trimmers. What is your view?

I have seen trials of roses pruned in this way and, quite frankly, they look hideous. I do not believe the claims that the frayed shoots do not serve as entry points for diseases, and it is a practice that I would never recommend or contemplate.

I have heard New English Roses being recommended. What are they and should I prune them like other shrub roses?

The New English Roses are an entirely new group of roses which were produced by the rose breeder David Austin to combine the flower form and fragrance of the old shrub varieties with the longer flowering period of modern roses. They are mostly double flowered, have good weather tolerance and make excellent plants for modern gardens.

I find that they respond to two types of pruning. They can be given the same pruning regime I use with almost all my other shrub roses – that is, very little. Each year I cut out any damaged, dying or diseased shoots to a few centimetres above soil level, and every two or three years I cut out one or two of the largest, thickest and oldest shoots in order to encourage regular shoot renewal.

These roses are, however, also amenable to being pruned like modern floribunda (cluster-flowered) cultivars. Each year cut out any dead, damaged, feeble or dying shoots to a few centimetres above soil level. Then cut back, also to just above soil level, the oldest one-third of the shoots and cut back the remaining shoots by one-third of their length.

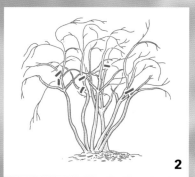

PRUNING A CLEMATIS

1 GROUP 1 CLEMATIS
Simply tidy up any straggly growths and cut back any dead stems to just above a node.

2 GROUP 2 CLEMATIS
Cut out dead or damaged shoots and cut back the remainder by about 30cm (12in).

3 GROUP 3 CLEMATIS
Cut back all growth to about 75cm (30in) above soil level.

I tried pruning all my clematis in the same way and it seemed to work. Are the experts wrong?

No, the experts are not wrong. There is a difference between obtaining the optimum performance from your plants and obtaining an adequate performance, and I would suggest that your clematis would have been even better if you had pruned them correctly.

Following is a simple pruning regime for clematis; note that all pruning is done in early spring and that pruning time relates to flowering time.

❁ **GROUP 1** *(clematis that flower early in the year)*

Prune them immediately after flowering by cutting back all weak and dead stems to just above a node. Any tangled or excessive growth should also be cut back, but large, well-established plants that are growing where they may be allowed free rein need not be pruned at all. Conversely, a plant that has become a tangled mass may be pruned back as hard as a Group 2 or even a Group 3 plant and will regenerate successfully, although all of one year's flower buds will, of course, be removed.

❁ **GROUP 2** *(clematis that flower early in the summer)*

Like Group 1 clematis, they should be pruned by cutting out any dead or weak stems. As they flower rather later than Group 1 clematis, however, follow the maxim that they require rather harder pruning and cut back the remaining shoots by about 30cm (12in), cutting to just above a pair of plump buds. Any dead leaf stalks should be trimmed away and the plant generally tidied up.

❁ **GROUP 3** *(clematis that flower later in the summer)*

These plants should be pruned much more severely. All of the previous season's growth should be cut back to just above a pair of plump buds positioned about 75cm (30in) above soil level. If there is so much top growth that it will be blown around in the winter, however, the bulk may be cut back in late autumn, leaving the final tidying until the following spring.

ABOVE: The vigorous, early-flowering *Clematis montana* needs little regular pruning.

How should I prune my tree peony?

The short answer is that you should not. The name 'tree peony' is a misnomer for these are simply medium sized or large shrubs – *Paeonia delavayi, P. x lemoinei, P. lutea, P. potaninii, P. suffruticosa* (moutan) and their hybrids are usually so called. They are classic examples of plants that require no pruning and tend to suffer from die-back if they are subjected to any.

ABOVE: Tree peonies are beautiful when in flower; but they aren't, in fact, trees, and they shouldn't be pruned.

After several years, my climbers all seem to be performing badly. Will pruning help?

It might, but it is a mistake to imagine that pruning is the answer to all plants' ills. Climbing plants often suffer as much from incorrect training as from incorrect pruning, and it is often the case that a plant that has been neglected in one respect has probably been neglected in others, too, and feeding and pest and disease control may also have been ignored.

The commonest failure in the training of climbing plants, especially roses, is that the shoots have all been allowed to grow vertically and, in consequence, all the flowers are borne at the top.

If at least some branches are trained horizontally, flower buds will develop along the length of each stem and a much more attractive effect will result when the plant flowers from top to bottom.

Containers

ABOVE: It's important to choose a container that is in proportion to the size of your plant.

What depth and diameter of tub do you recommend for larger plants?

When large shrubs and small trees are going to be grown in containers in the long term it makes sense to repot them as infrequently as possible, partly because the bigger a plant is, the more likely it is to suffer as a result of the disturbance, and partly because it is a heavy and difficult operation. You should, therefore, choose a large container from the very start, and I would suggest one that is about 60cm (24in) in diameter and depth.

It is at the other end of the size spectrum that I think you will have more serious problems, because gardeners frequently use containers that are too small to work properly. In any container with a diameter less than about 20cm (8in), the frequency with which you have to water will become a serious nuisance. By the same token, small, flat-sided containers for hanging on walls also suffer from very rapid drying out.

Which potting compost should I use for growing plants in containers?

Your choice of compost will depend entirely on how long you think that the plants will be in the containers. Apart from hanging baskets, where weight considerations dictate that a light, soil-less compost is to be preferred, I like to use a soil-based compost in containers. The ideal is the well-tried John Innes formula, which is obtainable as Numbers 1, 2 and 3. These numbers reflect the increasing fertilizer content in each of the formulations, and this serves to indicate the length of time over which they will be effective. For short-term, temporary growing, therefore, use No. 1; for plants such as summer bedding, which will be grown in a single season, use No. 2; and for semi-permanent plants, such as shrubs, use No. 3. Remember, however, that the nutrient content of No. 3 will be depleted over time and supplementary feeding will be necessary.

I have lost two wooden tubs through rotting. How can I save the last one?

Wooden half-barrel tubs do make excellent plant containers, but I have experienced the same problem, and even if the timber is heavily impregnated with preservative, contact with the compost means that you will be lucky if it lasts for more than about six years.

The solution is simple, however : line the tub with plastic sheet (black is the least obtrusive), taking care, of course, to make a few drainage holes in the sheet to coincide with those in the tub itself.

ABOVE: Wooden half-barrels are a relatively inexpensive form of large container.

LEFT: Lead or even replica lead containers really are the ultimate for plant display.

Is it true that an old lead urn cannot be used as a container because it will poison the plants?

It is just possible that new lead could cause very slight problems to some sensitive plants, and it might be wise to allow it to weather for one season. Old lead presents no such problem, however, and offers some of the most beautiful (if expensive) options for container gardening.

Trees for containers
There are several hardy trees that will grow happily in a container:

* *Acer palmatum* var. *dissectum*
* *Acer palmatum* 'Red Pygmy'
* *Cupressus macrocarpa* 'Goldcrest'
* *Cupressus sempervirens* Stricta Group
* *Juniperus scopulorum* 'Blue Heaven'
* *Laurus nobilis* (bay)
* *Taxus baccata* 'Standishii'

Yes, and it is well worth carrying out such repairs. Modern epoxy resins work very well, but you must make sure that the surfaces are clean and dry before you apply the glue. With large and valuable containers that have major cracks or breaks, it is worth supplementing the glue with non-ferrous wire, discreetly secured around the pot below the rim.

Top Left: This winter-flowering basket with pansies and heathers shows that hanging baskets can be year-round attractions.

Bottom Left: Nasturtiums are very much more wind tolerant than you might imagine.

Can you suggest some tough plants that are suitable for a hanging basket in a windy spot?

It is often forgotten that by putting plants in a hanging basket you are exposing them to the elements, especially the wind, to a much greater extent than when they are in containers at ground level. This is true of all hanging baskets at all times, but it is especially important if your garden is already windy and exposed and, of course, if you are planting a hanging basket for winter use. Following are my top plants for both winter and summer hanging baskets for a windy location:

SUMMER BASKETS:
- *Begonia* Non Stop Series; *B. semperflorens* Cultorum group
- *Brachyscome* spp. (Swan river daisy)
- *Calceolaria integrifolia* 'Sunshine'
- *Diascia barberae* 'Ruby Field'
- *Fuchsia* cvs.
- *Helichrysum petiolare*
- *Impatiens* cvs. (busy Lizzie)
- *Lobelia* cvs.
- *Lysimachia nummularia* (creeping Jenny)
- *Nemesia strumosa*
- *Tropaeolum* cvs. (nasturtium)
- *Verbena* cvs.
- *Viola* cvs. (violas and summer-flowering pansies)

WINTER BASKETS:
- *Ajuga reptans* (bugle)
- Dwarf conifers, such as *Juniperus communis* 'Compressa' and *J. squamata* 'Blue Star'
- *Euonymus* spp. (spindle tree)
- *Hedera* spp. (ivy)
- *Lamium galeobdolon* (yellow archangel); *L. maculatum* (dead nettle)
- *Senecio cineraria* (syn. *Cineraria maritima*)
- *Thymus* spp. (thyme)
- *Tolmeia menziesii* (thousand mothers)
- *Vinca major* (greater periwinkle)
- *Viola* cvs. (winter-flowering pansy)

What type of hanging basket liner do you recommend?

There are several liners available for hanging baskets, including natural sphagnum moss, artificial liners made commercially from sphagnum moss or liners of similar texture that are made from recycled wool or other natural fibres. If you are using natural sphagnum, however, it is very important not to collect it yourself from local bogs or woodland. Sphagnum is now grown commercially for harvesting, and the moss sold at garden centres comes from these sources.

You will see rigid liners for sale made from various compressed materials, including paper and cardboard, but I find them much less satisfactory, because they never look as attractive as moss; it is not always easy to cut holes for planting and the sharp edges of the holes can damage plants as you push them through; and they have no water-absorbing capacity.

ABOVE: I have been very impressed with some of the modern fibre linings for hanging baskets.

How can I minimize the amount of watering for my hanging basket?

Using an absorbent liner (see above) will help, but you should also use a compost specially formulated for hanging baskets. These now generally contain small water-absorbing granules, which release the moisture over a period of time and serve to reduce watering frequency by at least half.

The ideal system, however, is a drip watering system. These need to be planned in advance and they use essentially the same equipment as that sold for use in greenhouses. A system of tiny plastic tubes, one to each hanging basket or other container, is connected to a water reservoir or to the water mains. The attention needed is almost negligible although you must still add liquid fertilizer manually. If you add this to the water reservoir, algal growth will soon build up in the narrow tubes and block them. Once a year, after use, the equipment should be taken apart and cleaned.

RIGHT: A mixed planting of pelargoniums is delightful, but takes time to create.

Drainage

Container-grown plants are very vulnerable to water-logging. All containers must have drainage holes in the base. Cover the holes with crocks so that compost is not washed out, and then add a layer of drainage material such as gravel. Wherever possible, raise containers from the ground so that excess water can drain away freely. This is particularly important in winter, when standing water might freeze around a plant's roots.

I have several tubs of pelargoniums, which I raised from seed, but all have failed to flower. What did I do wrong?

My guess is that the plants have not had a sufficiently long season, although just how long depends mainly on the temperatures in which they are grown. There are two ways to achieve reliable flowering – sowing seed in late summer or late winter – but careful calculations and trials by commercial growers (who know better than amateur gardeners about cost-effectiveness) have shown that late summer sowing is to be preferred. If the seeds are sown then, you will have strong plants by early winter. They can then be kept relatively cool until the spring and still flower in early summer. If the seeds are not sown until late winter, much higher temperatures (and hence higher costs) are required to produce good plants in time for the new season.

Sow the seeds about 5mm (¼in) deep in a soil-based seedling compost in a pot or seed tray. The optimum germination temperature is about 22°C (72°F), and at this level the seed should germinate within seven days. Once germination has occurred, the temperature should be lowered to around 18°C (64°F), and after about two more weeks the plants should be pricked out to individual pots, just as with the cuttings. They may then be grown in these pots at a minimum temperature of 7°C (45°F) through the winter.

ABOVE: Potatoes grow well in deep containers and can give you a small but very early crop.

Is it true that potatoes can be grown in a tub?

Yes, they can. You will never be self-sufficient in potatoes if you grow them this way, but you can certainly gain much pleasure and satisfaction from a small, very early crop. Obviously, as the potato is a large plant, you will need a large container. The best results are achieved with plastic dustbins with drainage holes punched in the base. Remember that a container of such a large size, filled with compost, will be extremely heavy, so choose its position carefully and don't try to move it again. Any good quality potting compost will suffice. Fill the container at least two weeks before planting to allow the contents to settle and plant the seed tubers 20cm (8in) apart. From then on, it will be a matter of protecting the young shoots from frost as they emerge, of watering regularly and copiously (the compost must not become waterlogged but must not dry out either) and of giving a liquid feed once a week from the time that the plants are about 20cm (8in) tall. And when you harvest the first tubers, no potato will ever have tasted as good.

I have been told that roses and some other plants cannot be grown in containers. Is this correct?

No, any plant can be grown in a container, and the only constraint is the size of the container. The biggest difficulties arise with plants that have a shallow, fibrous root system (like many conifers), because the compost dries out at the surface and they suffer in consequence, and also those, like roses, that have a long tap root. These plants require a pot that is proportionately deep because they too are intolerant of drying out at the surface and must have moisture at depth on which they draw.

LEFT: Although miniature roses grow well in containers, larger varieties require proportionately deeper containers.

Can I replant a container at the end of the summer using the same compost?

Sometimes, but with some rather important provisos. The compost that you will have used for your summer plants will inevitably be seriously depleted in nutrients by the end of the season. If you have used a soil-less compost, there will be almost no nutrient at all, and even if you have been topping up with liquid fertilizer, what little remains will be in imbalance. So soil-less composts (and that includes those in growing bags) should be rejected and dug into the garden as a soil improver.

If you have used a soil-based compost and provided that the plants growing in it have been free from pests and diseases, you should remove the top 10cm (4in) and replace this with fresh before replanting. In large containers, it is clearly impractical and uneconomic to refill the entire volume of compost every season and this partial replacement, or top-dressing, provides a satisfactory solution.

I have an eight-year-old camellia in a tub, and this year it produced only two miserable flowers. Why?

The reason is almost certainly because you have failed to feed the camellia adequately. The best way to ensure that container-grown plants continue to flower is not to repot them because they need to be under slight stress in order to bloom satisfactorily. This advice should not be taken to extremes, however, and if a plant is not to be repotted, it should be given a fertilizer with a relatively high potash content. A once-a-season application of a proprietary rose fertilizer should be routine for all flowering shrubs in containers, and if they are fairly vigorous plants (which camellias are not), this may be usefully supplemented by a soluble fertilizer, such as tomato feed, during the growing season.

RIGHT: Camellias are excellent container plants but must be given the right conditions.

I use leafmould in my containers. Does it contain harmful pests and diseases?

No, leafmould contains nothing serious, although it often harbours woodlice. This query begs the question of whether you are using leafmould in the best way, however. It is an invaluable organic substance, and garden leaves should not be allowed to go to waste. But, with one or two exceptions, leafmould is not ideal for use in containers. It is put to far better use as a mulch on garden borders, and the only time I use it in containers is on lilies, which seem to derive especial benefit from it. Every year, I use leafmould to which I have added a little bonemeal as an autumn top dressing on my pots of lilies, applying a layer about 5cm (2in) deep.

My azalea in a tub has pale, sickly looking leaves. What is the matter with it?

This is always likely to happen with plants that require an acidic growing medium. Over a period of time, especially if you have been using 'hard' tapwater, the build-up of alkaline salts in the compost will prevent the plants from being able to absorb iron. This means, in turn, that they will be unable to manufacture chlorophyll and will turn yellow in consequence. Always try to use rainwater for these plants and, as a corrective treatment, apply a fertilizer containing sequestered iron.

ABOVE: Given the right compost and correct care, azaleas can be stunning container plants.

Paths, patios, paving &
hard landscaping

I have heard of bark chippings recommended as a path material. Does it attract pests and diseases?

ABOVE: Bark chippings make a very effective, mud-free path with a truly rural feel.

No, not if you use properly prepared material. There are various grades of shredded bark, and you need coarse chips for paths. Cheap material often contains woody debris, which includes unpleasant splinters. There should be no disease problems in bark that can spread to your garden, and although it may provide hiding places for woodlice, it is most unlikely to have any impact on the overall incidence of garden pests. I have used bark paths for years without problems of any kind.

I would love to have attractive paving on my patio. Can you suggest something that will not be prohibitively expensive?

There is no doubt that some paving materials are costly, but if you choose carefully it is always possible to select something that will be within your budget. There is now a huge range of materials to choose from and I have summarized the features of each.

Bricks can be laid in a variety of attractive designs, of which the herringbone is my own favourite. Choose brick for a town garden or for a country garden where the house is brick built. But don't use old standard building bricks, which crack and crumble quickly after frosts. Hard engineering bricks or purpose-made concrete replicas are much better.

For a stone-built house, stone slabs will always look right, but real York or other paving stones are now prohibitively expensive. Instead, use one of the excellent modern replicas, which are much easier to lay because they are of uniform thickness. Terracotta paving tiles, which mimic old worn patterns, are also now available and are extremely attractive. Always be aware that any uneven surface, whether intentional or not, will cause endless frustration when you stand garden furniture on it.

Concrete is relatively inexpensive and relatively quick to lay. It can look very dull, however, although the surface can be enlivened and also made less slippery by brushing it coarsely before it dries.

Wood is less commonly used for a patio but is used to create decking (see page 150).

ABOVE: Modern paving materials mean that attractive steps and courtyards can be created relatively inexpensively.

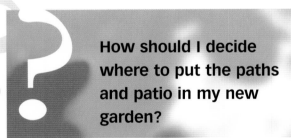

How should I decide where to put the paths and patio in my new garden?

This is an area of garden design where I feel that theory falls down most often and where there is no substitute for the practical common sense of the garden owner. It is all too easy to sit down with a piece of squared paper, look at the overall dimensions of a garden plot and decide where the various paths and paved areas should be. When this is done, however, practicalities can easily be overlooked, and there is no better way to make more realistic decisions than by standing in the garden at intervals during the day and seeing where the sun falls at the times you are most likely to want to be sitting out. That should determine where your patio goes. The siting of paths is best done by watching the routes that people take naturally to walk to different parts of the garden over a period of weeks or, if you have time, months. Place your paths accordingly.

Building a patio

When you are deciding where to site a patio, consider what it is going to be used for. If you enjoy entertaining, you will need to have good access to and from the kitchen and also ample room for a table and chairs. It is both uncomfortable and potentially dangerous if there is insufficient room to push chairs back from the table and for the cook to move easily around it.

Decking is all the rage now. What do you think of it?

I heartily dislike decking and feel that it is one of the gardening fads that we could happily do without. It seems to have been foisted on us by the people who undertake television make-over programmes because it is the easiest way to cover a large section of a garden in a very short time – which is, after all, the principle behind the make-over concept – but it has nothing at all to do with gardening.

Decking is an appalling waste of good growing space. The average size of a garden today is less than 200 square metres (just over 2000 square feet), so it is difficult to imagine why anyone thinks we should cover it up with wooden boards, least of all with wooden boards painted in bright colours. Decking is the stuff of stage sets and places to moor boats. In a real garden it very quickly becomes both unsightly and downright dangerous – try walking over wooden boards after a winter's rain and algae have had a go at it. If you are determined to cover up some of your garden, think about using gravel instead (see page 153).

RIGHT: Decking is fine for flower-show display gardens but is not really suitable not for real life.

I like the idea of brick paving but I'm told it won't survive the frost. Is this true?

Brick paving is absolutely superb in the places where gravel is not suitable, and this is the type of path that I have had laid in my own kitchen garden. It is, however, perfectly true that normal house bricks will not survive the frost when they are laid directly on the ground and can soak up moisture from the soil.

There are two alternatives. Blue engineering bricks work very well, but they have the drawbacks that they are blue, not red, and also that to buy and have them laid professionally is an expensive undertaking. There is now a very much better solution. Many paving companies manufacture remarkably convincing replicas from concrete, sometimes as individual bricks but also as blocks, generally of four or six, arranged in different patterns. These are simple to lay although they should always be bedded on hardcore. After a year or so they are almost indistinguishable from the real thing and at a fraction of the price.

LEFT: Replica bricks reduce the cost of creating brick paving in terms of both materials and labour.

ABOVE: Gravel is perhaps the easiest of all paving materials to lay.

Gravel looks terrific, but how can I stop it sticking to my boots?

Gravel is terrific: it is cheap and adaptable and simplicity itself to lay. You should not use it everywhere in the garden, however, and it is certainly not appropriate in places where you will regularly be walking straight from the soil on to the path. In effect, this means that it should not be used in the vegetable garden. In other places, among borders and permanent plantings, it works extremely well, and I have had gravel paths in much of my garden for many years with no problems or frustrations. I find that it needs topping up about every three years and there really is little to choose between rounded pea gravel and angular stone chips.

It is sometimes suggested that it should be laid over purpose-made porous plastic membrane to keep down weed growth, but although this is ideal for a large gravelled area, I don't like it under paths because it can make them slippery.

I don't like using chemicals. How can I prevent weeds from appearing in my paths?

Before I give my answer, it is worth pointing out that modern path weedkillers don't have the unpleasant effects of older products, such as sodium chlorate, which was notorious for seeping into the soil of beds nearby and damaging plants. But clearly, by its nature, a path weedkiller must persist if it is to achieve its effects. I have found that manufacturers' claims that they are a once-a-year treatment are seldom correct, however, and two applications are needed – evidence, indeed, that the persistence is fairly short-lived. If you really wish to avoid all chemicals, however, try the following options, the first of which requires pre-planning:

- Lay a plastic membrane under the path before you lay it; for reasons I have given on page 151, I don't like to use this under gravel but it could certainly be put beneath slabs or bricks.
- Make sure that the cracks and gaps between paving slabs are well mortared.
- Use mat-forming plants, such as *Thymus serpyllum* (thyme) and *Mentha requienii* (Corsican mint), which will readily establish in the cracks between paving and are pretty effective at suppressing weed growth.
- Use a hooked weeding tool to remove weeds by hand.

ABOVE: Path weeds can be controlled effectively with weed-killers; but there are other options

PLANTING IN GRAVEL
Cut a cross shape in the underlying plastic sheet and peel back the corners to create a planting hole.

How can I keep my paths clear of green slime without killing my plants?

The green slime is algal growth and it can be kept at bay by periodic use of one of the proprietary path-clearing chemicals. Some contain the moss killer and algicide dichlorophen, while others are very dilute mineral acids. All should be used exactly as the manufacturers direct, but they will not 'creep' into the soil nearby. Never use bleach on paths; it is extremely dangerous and will certainly damage plants if it is splashed on to them.

What is a gravel garden?
My gravel path has weeds
in it; does this count?

No, it does not. I think that using gravel is one of the most undervalued ways of creating an attractive area of garden that is both striking and easy to maintain. In addition, unlike decking (see page 150), gravel sits easily in the European gardening tradition. In effect, it is nothing more than an area of soil over which a gravel mulch has been laid, but, unlike organic mulches, it does not decompose. In reality, it should be a little more than that, of course, but even so it remains a very simple and inexpensive feature.

Thoroughly dig your chosen area and work in plenty of organic matter; this is not something you will be able to do again. Level the area and then lay porous plastic membrane over the surface (this is the membrane that I do not recommend for gravel paths; see page 151). This will keep the whole area weed free and yet allow rain and fertilizer to penetrate. Then add a layer 5cm (2in) deep of your chosen gravel or stone chippings over the surface. It doesn't matter greatly what you choose, but I prefer to use stone that matches whatever occurs locally: limestone in a limestone area, granite in a granite area, for example. Remember that the types of plant you can grow will be determined to some degree by the type of stone you use – you cannot, for instance, grow acid-loving species if you have a limestone gravel bed.

Following are the top five plants from my own gravel garden, which tolerate moderate acidity and alkalinity, to get you started, but do feel free to experiment:

* *Crocus chrysanthus* 'Ladykiller' – a white and purple, spring-flowering bulb
* *Felicia amelloides* 'Santa Anita' (blue daisy)
* *Genista lydia* – a yellow-flowered, low-growing shrub
* *Geranium orientalitibeticum* – a ground-cover geranium with mottled foliage
* *Salix repens* – a creeping willow with grey and yellow upright catkins
* *Stipa arundinacea* (pheasant's tail grass) – an ornamental grass

Glossary

Alpine Vague term for plants growing naturally in mountainous areas (not necessarily the Alps).

Ammonium sulphate The most valuable and widely used artificial fast-acting nitrogen fertilizer; used in the artificial fertilizer mixture Growmore.

Annual A plant that completes the cycle from seed to seed within a single season. Divided into hardy and half-hardy annuals.

Bacterium (pl. bacteria) Simple organisms that play a vital role in the breakdown and recycling of organic matter. Some cause important diseases of plants and animals.

Bark A protective corky layer of dead cells on the outside of older stems and roots of woody plants.

Bed Vague term for a planted area; often used to describe an area of annual plants as distinct from a border which contains perennials.

Biennial A plant that requires two seasons to complete the cycle from seed to seed. Generally, biennials flower in the first year and set seed in the next.

Biological control The control of plant pests by using an organism that is a natural parasite or predator.

Bonemeal Fertilizer derived from ground animal bones. A valuable source of phosphate and a small amount of nitrogen.

Budding Form of grafting where the scion comprises a single bud and enables a large number of plants to be produced from limited material.

Bulb A vegetative reproduction and storage organ comprising a very short stem (the basal plate) from which the roots arise, with a mass of swollen, overlapping immature leaves.

Canker A disease of woody plants where there is localized and gradually extending death of the cells beneath the bark resulting in a characteristic target-like lesion.

Carbon The most important chemical element in living organisms and an essential component of all organic chemical compounds.

Carbon dioxide Colourless, odourless gas as present in the air and essential for plant life as it is one of the raw materials for photosynthesis.

Chlorophyll Green pigment in plants that traps energy from sunlight to facilitate the process of photosynthesis.

Clay One of the three major divisions of the mineral components of soil. Clay particles are especially important because they attract and hold plant nutrients.

Cloche Glass or plastic cloches placed over plants will provide protection and added warmth, so allowing extensions of growing time at the beginning and end of the season.

Clone A group of individuals that are genetically identical, like potato and apple varieties, having been produced by asexual rather than sexual reproduction.

Cold frame A glazed frame used for hardening off plants before they are put outdoors and for growing such crops as melons and cucumbers with enhanced warmth.

Compost Garden compost is the part decomposed remains of garden waste and is a valuable soil amendment. Seedling and potting composts are mixtures for growing plants in containers. They are divided into soil-based John Innes composts, and soil-less composts. All have fertilizer added to enable plants to be grown for some time before additional feeding is needed.

Corm A vegetative reproduction and storage organ comprising a swollen stem base with buds in the axils of the scale-like leaf remains of the previous season.

Cotyledon Also called a seed leaf; leaves that form part of the embryo of a plant within the seed.

Cultivar A variety of a plant that has arisen, either deliberately or by accident, in cultivation.

Cuttings Short pieces of stem or root cut from a parent plant and induced to form roots in order to grow into a daughter plant.

Damping off Disease of seedlings and young plants, best avoided by using healthy seed, new compost and clean pots and trays.

Dead-heading The removal of the faded flowerheads of ornamental plants; an important task because it stimulates new flowerbuds to develop and also removes potential infection points for diseases.

Deciduous plant One that loses and replaces all of its leaves annually.

Dicotyledon One of the two main groups of flowering plants, characterized by having two cotyledons emerge from the germinating seed.

Dried blood Organic fertilizer used as fairly quick-acting source of nitrogen.

Evergreen plant One that loses its leaves piecemeal over a long period; the individual leaves do not however last forever.

F1 hybrid The offspring from the crossing of two inbred parents. F1 hybrids have become very important in commercial horticulture because of their uniformity and generally larger size and greater vigour.

F2 hybrid The offspring from allowing the members of an F1 population to cross among themselves. Generally less vigorous and less uniform but cheaper than F1 hybrids.

Family A grouping of plants containing similar genera.

Fern Non-flowering green plant, reproducing by means of spores but having fairly advanced conducting and other tissues. Many species are widely used in gardens for their ability to grow in damp moist places and for the attractiveness of their leaves or fronds.

Fertilization The union of male and female cells to produce offspring; the essence of sexual reproduction and, in plants, follows as a consequence of pollination. Also used in gardening to mean the application of fertilizer to soil or plants.

Fertilizer Plant nutrient applied artificially by gardeners. Often divided into artificial fertilizers, produced in a chemical factory, and organic fertilizers, derived from a naturally occurring source.

Fish, blood and bone Popular general purpose fertilizer containing bonemeal, fishmeal and dried blood.

Fungus (pl. fungi) An organism lacking chlorophyll, reproducing by spores and composed of a mass of microscopic filamentous threads called hyphae. Many cause important plant diseases but are also vital in the decay of organic matter in compost and soil.

Genetic engineering The artificial alteration of the DNA of plant or animal cells with, among others, the objective of making improvements that would otherwise be impossible or could be achieved only after many generations of conventional breeding.

Genus (pl. genera) A classificatory group containing closely related species; similar genera are themselves grouped into a family.

Germination The process by which seeds or spores produce new growth and develop into new individuals. Commonly, a period of dormancy takes place after the formation of the seed or spore and certain conditions are then needed to break this dormancy.

Grafting Technique in which two different plants, often of different variety or even species are artificially induced to grow as one. A length of stem (the

scion) of one plant is inserted into the rooted part (stock) of another. An invaluable method of propagating plants that have some horticulturally desirable feature but inefficient rooting.

Growmore Balanced general purpose artificial fertilizer containing N:P:K in the ratio 7:7:7.

Growth hormone Chemical that controls the way in which plant cells and tissues grow and become differentiated; sometimes known as auxins.

Half-hardy Term to describe a plant that is sufficiently hardy to grow outdoors in a temperate-climate summer but will not withstand frost.

Hardening off Process by which plants are accustomed gradually to outdoor conditions after being raised in warmth. Even very hardy plants require hardening off under these circumstances.

Hardy Able to tolerate frost.

Herb Popularly used to mean a plant with medicinal or culinary flavouring properties but also used to mean any non-woody flowering plant.

Herbaceous perennial Perennial plant with no woody structure, therefore unlike a shrub. Contrary to popular belief, not all are deciduous and die down in the autumn; a considerable number are evergreen and may therefore need some winter protection.

Herbicide Weedkiller, a chemical to kill weeds.

Hoof and horn Organic fertilizer derived from ground-up animal remains, valuable as a slow-release form of nitrogen.

Humus Part decomposed organic matter, especially when integrated within the soil.

Hybrid Offspring from genetically unlike parents.

Insecticide Chemical to kill insects; some are also effective against mites, woodlice and other garden pests.

John Innes compost Soil-based composts (John Innes is not a brand name but a type of compost) and still the standards. There are four commonly available: Seed, and Potting Nos. 1, 2, and 3 with increasing amounts of fertilizer for increasingly long-term plant growth.

Larva (pl. larvae) Immature form of an animal which develops into a physically very different adult by metamorphosis.

Lawn sand A blend of ferrous sulphate (moss and weedkiller), ammonium sulphate (fertilizer) and sand (inert bulk).

Layering Method of propagating plants by pegging a horizontal shoot into the soil and leaving it undisturbed until it forms roots. It is then severed from the parent.

Leaf Plant organ in which most photosynthesis takes place. Leaves may be modified to form hooks, tendrils and other structures for secondary roles.

Loam Soil containing approximately equal amounts of clay, sand and silt; an ideal all-round growing medium.

Manure Imprecise term for animal excrement especially used as soil amendment and plant nutrient; as distinct from the term compost, which is generally used for decomposed plant remains.

Mildew One of two distinct and superficially similar but quite unrelated types of plant disease-causing fungi, known as downy mildews and powdery mildews.

Monocotyledons One of the two main groups of flowering plants, characterized by having one cotyledon emerge from the germinating seed. Monocotyledons generally have long, typically grass-like leaves by contrast with the relatively small, more or less rounded leaves of dicotyledons.

Moss Evolutionarily primitive green bryophyte plant reproducing by spores and related to liverworts.

Mould Imprecise term for a fungal growth.

Mulch Material laid over the soil surface in order to conserve moisture and suppress weeds. Most commonly compost, leafmould, bark or some other organic matter is used, but plastic sheet is sometimes employed also.

Nitrate Salt of nitric acid and the form in which many nitrogen-containing fertilizers are applied to soil or plants.

Nitrogen Chemical element and the single most important plant nutrient, being a major constituent of protein. Nitrogen is readily washed from the soil and regular applications may be needed in gardens therefore.

NPK fertilizer Fertilizer containing the three major plant nutrients. These are nitrogen (N), phosphorus (P) and potassium (K).

Organic gardening A confusing term. It tends to be used to refer to gardening practices that have (or are believed to have) no adverse effect on the environment (are 'environmentally friendly').

Peat Dead plant material, often many thousands of years old, that has only partially decomposed through lying in waterlogged conditions (commonly called bogs). There are two main types of peat, moss or sphagnum peat, which is brown and highly acidic, and fen peat, which is black and less acidic, and may even be alkaline. Because of the despoiling of valuable natural habitats by peat extraction, there has been a concerted campaign to find alternative, sustainable materials for the preparation of horticultural potting composts.

Perennial A plant that lives for more than two seasons. Many plants grown as half-hardy annuals in temperate climates are perennial in their native habitats.

pH Potential of hydrogen, a measure indicating the concentration of hydrogen ions (charged atoms) in a solution. In practice, a measure of relative acidity or alkalinity on a logarithmic scale from 0 (extremely acidic) to 14 (extremely alkaline). The mid-point 7 is called neutral. Most garden soils lie between pH 5 and 7.5.

Phosphate Salt of phosphoric acid and the form in which the element phosphate is taken up by plants from the soil.

Photosynthesis The formation of organic chemical compounds by green plants from carbon dioxide and water using the green pigment chlorophyll.

Pollination The transfer of pollen from a male anther to a female stigma on either the same or different flowers as a prelude to fertilization.

Potash Everyday term for potassium salt, especially potassium oxide, an important fertilizer.

Potassium Chemical element and major plant nutrient, especially important for flower and fruit production and a significant ingredient therefore of such mixtures as tomato fertilizers.

Pricking out The transfer of seedlings from a seed tray to their growing positions.

Propagation The multiplication of plants artificially, using either vegetative means (cuttings, division or layering for example) or natural reproductive processes (seeds).

Propagator Someone who propagates or, more commonly, a piece of equipment to facilitate propagation. In general, a device to maintain a moist environment is essential, whatever the method of propagation, and basic propagators are seed trays with a ventilated cover. As enhanced warmth is important for most types of propagation, many propagators incorporate a heating element.

Pruning The artificial removal of parts of plants in order to improve their shape or productivity. It's a mistake to imagine that pruning is limited to trees and shrubs; the dead-heading of annuals is a version of pruning.

Rhizome A thick, usually horizontal underground stem that facilitates the spread of plants through the soil and which may also form a food storage and perennating body.

Ring culture Greenhouse system of growing tomatoes and other plants in compost in bottomless pots placed on a gravel bed and fed with liquid fertilizer. It offers a relatively pest- and disease-free growing system.

Root Serves two main functions in plants: to provide physical stability and to provide the medium for the uptake of water and mineral nutrients from the soil. In modified form roots also provide storage for food reserves. In a few plants, roots may be aerial and extract moisture and nutrients from the air and provide support for climbers.

Rootstock A plant that is grown specifically for some attribute of its roots and on to which another variety is grafted. Rootstocks are commonly used with garden plants that have good flowering or fruiting ability but weak root systems.

Rotation The changing of the places where particular crops are grown in successive years. It is used especially with vegetables which in gardens are generally grown on a three-course rotation (any one crop on the same site once every three years). The principle is to minimize the build-up of pests and diseases and utilize the full range of soil nutrients but in gardens, unlike commercial horticulture, the small distance between plots means that the benefits are fairly limited.

Scion Part of plant (usually stem or bud) inserted into the rooted part of another plant (the stock or rootstock) in order to form a union or graft.

Secateur Also called pruner, a small cutting tool for pruning, embodying two slicing blades (bypass or scissor action) or a single blade cutting against a blunt surface (anvil pattern).

Seed The characteristic reproductive body of seed plants, the product of a fertilized ovule; commonly contained within a fruit.

Seedling Plant newly emerged from a seed.

Shrubbery The dedicated shrubbery is seen less in modern gardens than the mixed planting of shrubs and herbaceous perennials. The days of the sombre 19th-century shrubbery of evergreen foliage shrubs have in any event largely been replaced by mixed plantings of deciduous and evergreen, flowering and foliage types.

Soil The top-most layer of the land surface, usually divided into topsoil and sub soil, and the key to all gardening activities. It is important to understand, however, that while containing inert, mineral components of differing sizes and chemical compositions, it is also a dynamic medium. It changes as organic matter is added and decomposes, as plants take up nutrients and as the numerous living inhabitants influence it in their own ways, both beneficial and detrimental to plant life.

Species (note that the word has no singular) A collection of individual organisms that are readily able to breed among themselves but not generally able to breed with organisms belong to other species.

Spore Microscopic reproductive structure of many organisms, including fungi, ferns, mosses, liverworts and some bacteria. Very different from a seed and a general term used for a wide range of bodies that are themselves produced in a wide variety of ways, some following sexual and some asexual reproduction.

Stem Part of a plant bearing leaves, buds and flowers, normally green and aerial but may be variously modified. Some stems (rhizomes for example) are subterranean, others much abbreviated (the basal plate of a bulb) or swollen (potato tubers), but all are recognized and distinguished from roots or other organs by the presence of buds.

Stolon Horizontally-growing stem that roots at the nodes, as in a strawberry runner.

Stoma (pl. stomata) Pore in plant epidermis through which gas exchange with the air takes place.

Sub-species Abbreviated to ssp. or subsp., a group of individuals within a species that has developed slight (usually morphological or behavioural) differences, generally brought about by geographical isolation from the main species.

Sucker Modified plant root used to achieve adherence in self-clinging climbers.

Systemic Generally distributed within an organism. Used to describe the nature of infection by certain diseases or the mode of action of certain pesticides. Some of the most effective pesticides and fungicides are of systemic action but such chemicals take longer to clear from the tissues than contact chemicals so may lengthen the time before edible produce can be used.

Tilth The condition in which soil is suitable for plant growth.

Translocation The movement of chemicals within a plant. Important naturally as the means for the dispersion of nutrients but also taken advantage of by translocated weedkillers which reach otherwise inaccessible roots.

Transplanting The transfer of young plants, generally distinguished from pricking out in that the plants are at a more advanced stage of development before being moved.

Tuber Swollen storage organ which may be a modified root (dahlia) or stem (potato).

Variety Often used in the same sense as cultivar but its correct botanical meaning is a variant that has arisen in a plant species growing in the wild.

Virus Structurally simple organisms comprising a nucleic acid and one or more proteins. Absolute parasites in living within host cells.

Weed Familiarly, any native plant growing where it interferes with the efficient growing of a garden plant.

Index

Photographic Acknowledgements

Professor Stefan Buczacki
24 Top Left, 43, 44 Bottom Right, 47 Bottom, 52, 55 Bottom Left, 64, 66, 67, 68, 69 Bottom Left, 70, 82, 83 Top Left, 86, 90 Top Left, 95, 96–97 Bottom, 98 Bottom Right, 114–115, 116 Bottom Right, 137

Garden Picture Library
Mark Bolton 100, 127 Top Right, 129 Top Right, 138
Kathy Charlont 15 Bottom
Eric Crichton 123 Top
Ron Evans 49
Christopher Gallagher 40–41
John Glover 11, 46, 101 Top, 110, 148
Sunniva Harte 104, 145 Top
Marijke Heuff 139
Neil Holmes 33 Top Right, 33 Bottom Left
Michael Howes 17 Top, 73, 88, 90–91 Top, 93 Top, 120
Jacqui Hurst 81 Bottom
Lamontagne 125
Jane Legate 83 Bottom Right
Jane Legate 116 Top Left
Mayer/Le Scanff 18–19, 62, 71 Top Right, 103, 112, 129 Bottom Left
Zara McCalmot 113
Jerry Pavia 78
Howard Rice 12–13 Top, 18, 89, 101–102 Bottom, 119, 131 Top Right, 144
Alec Scaresbrook 149
John Ferro Sims 147
JS Sira 29 Top Right, 36 Bottom, 142 Top
Brigitte Thomas 31, 39, 65 Top Right
Juliette Wade 141 Top Right
Mel Watson 90–91 Bottom, 133 Top Right
Steve Wooster 94, 105, 145 Bottom, 153

Octopus Publishing Group Ltd.
Michael Boys 10–11, 42, 54, 75 Bottom, 79, 123 Bottom, 124 Bottom, 134 Bottom
Crockett 93 Bottom
Jerry Harpur 3 Centre, 12–13 Bottom, 15 Top, 16, 21, 25, 48 Top, 65 Bottom Left, 102, 114, 130, 151
Neil Holmes 38, 59, 74, 111
Andrew Lawson Front flap, 6, 20, 26, 34
Peter Myers 55 Top Right
Howard Rice 27 Bottom Right, 30 Bottom Left, 84–85 Top, 132, 133 Bottom Left, 134 Top
Gareth Lambidge Front Cover left, Front Cover right, Front Cover centre, Back Cover bottom centre
Steve Wooster 1, 3 left, 9 Bottom, 35, 50, 136, 140
George Wright 3 Right, 9 Top, 53, 63, 69 Top Right

Harpur Garden Library
28, 46–47, 61, 124–125, 127 Bottom Left
George Cooper 77
Susan Irvine 27 Top Left
Sheila McQeen 30 Top Right

Andrew Lawson
14 Bottom Left, 17 Bottom, 23, 29 Bottom Left, 32 Top Left, 36 Top, 48 Bottom, 51, 56, 78–79, 81 Top, 106 Top Right, 106 Bottom Right, 108, 117 Bottom Left, 118, 122, 126, 128, 131 Bottom Left, 141 Bottom Left, 142 Bottom, 150 Top Left, 150 Bottom Left
/Waterperry Gardens, Oxfordshire 24 Bottom Right

Photos Horticultural
8, 22, 36 Centre, 40, 44 Top Left, 45, 57, 58, 60, 71 Bottom Left, 72, 74–75 Top, 75 Top, 76, 76–77 Top, 80, 84–85 Bottom, 87, 96–97 Top, 98 Top Left, 99, 107, 109, 115, 117 Top Right, 121, 135, 143, 146, 152 J S Sira 14